Old-Time Recipes for
Home Made Wines

Old-Time Recipes for Home Made Wines Cordials and Liqueurs

From Fruits, Flowers, Vegetables, and Shrubs

Compiled by
Helen S. Wright

Fredonia Books
Amsterdam, The Netherlands

Old Time Recipes for Home Made
Wines Cordials and Liqueurs from
Fruits, Flowers, Vegetables and
Shrubs

by
Helen S. Wright

ISBN 1-58963-048-3

Reprinted from the 1909 edition

Fredonia Books
Amsterdam, The Netherlands
http://www.FredoniaBooks.com

I wish to acknowledge my indebtedness to the following books of reference: " The Compleat Housewife," " The Cook," " The Dictionary of Every-day Wants," " The Household Cyclopedia," " The Blue Grass Cook Book," " Two Hundred Recipes from French Cookery."

Old-Time Recipes for
Home Made Wines

Old=Time Recipes for
Home Made Wines

———◆———

INTRODUCTION

THE idea of compiling this little volume
occurred to me while on a visit to some
friends at their summer home in a quaint
New England village. The little town had
once been a thriving seaport, but now con-
sisted of hardly more than a dozen old-
fashioned Colonial houses facing each other
along one broad, well-kept street. A few
blind lanes led to less pretentious homes;
and still farther back farmhouses dotted the
landscape and broke the dead line of the
horizon.

For peace, contentment, and quiet seren-
ity of life, this little village might have
been Arcadia; the surrounding country, the
land of Beulah.

The ladies of the Great Houses, as the

villagers called the few Colonial mansions, were invariably spinsters or widows of uncertain years, the last descendants of a long line of sea captains and prosperous mariners, to whom the heritage of these old homes, rich with their time-honored furnishings and curios, served to keep warm the cockles of kindly hearts, which extended to the stranger that traditional hospitality which makes the whole world kin.

The social customs of this Adamless Eden were precise and formal. As with the dear ladies of Cranford, a call was a very serious affair, given and received with great gravity, and had its time limit set with strict punctuality. Cake and wine were invariably served as a preliminary warning toward early departure. Here came in my first acquaintance with many varieties of home-made wines, over whose wealth of color and delicacy of flavor my eyes and palate longed to linger.

Vulgar curiosity made me bold to inquire the names of a few; imagine my astonishment when graciously told that the gay dandelion, the modest daisy, the blushing currant, had one and all contributed their nectar to the joy of the occasion. Flattered by my interest, my gentle hostess broke strict rules of etiquette and invited me to linger, showing me rare old gardens aglow with flowers, fruits, and vegetables that in due time would contribute to their store, and at parting various time-worn recipes were urged upon me, with verbal instructions and injunctions upon the best methods of putting them to test.

From this beginning I ferreted out from other sources recipes for many curious concoctions, the very name of which fills the mind with fantasies and pictures of the long ago. Do we not feel poignant sympathy for the grief of the poor Widow of Malabar, whose flow of tears has descended in spirit, through three centuries, to those still faithful to her memory? Did we ever pause to consider what a slaughter of the innocents went to make famous many an old English tavern whose Sign of the Cock made the weary traveller pause and draw rein, and call loudly for the stirrup cup of this home-brewed ale? Can we not feel the ponderous presence, and smell the strong tobacco from the pipes of groups of stolid Dutchmen, of the days of Wouter Van Twiller, when we read of that one-time favorite beverage, Schiedam Schnapps? Again, are we not back in that dull, but delightful, society of the days of Colonel Newcome, when a quiet game of bezique was interrupted by the tidy servant who brought in the refreshing Orgeat and delicate seed cakes? Have not our own grandmothers boasted of the delicious flavor of old English Cowslip wine or Noyean Cordial?

I have confined myself exclusively to home-made beverages, gathering my fruits and flowers from old-fashioned, homely gardens. I leave to your imagination the times, fashions, and customs they recall. The aroma that clings to them is subtle. Age has blended and mellowed all that was crude in those bygone days.

With a gentle hand I tie my little bunch together and present you my bouquet.

THE best method of making these wines is to boil the ingredients, and ferment with yeast. Boiling makes the wine more soft and mellow. Some, however, mix the juice, or juice and fruit, with sugar and water unboiled, and leave the ingredients to ferment spontaneously. Your fruit should always be prime, and gathered dry, and picked clean from stalks, etc. The lees of wine are valuable for distillation, or making vinegar. When wine is put in the cask the fermentation will be renewed. Clear away the yeast as it rises, and fill up with wine, for which purpose a small quantity should be reserved. If brandy is to be added, it must be when the fermentation has nearly subsided, that is, when no more yeast is thrown up at the bung-hole, and when the hissing noise is not very perceptible; then mix a quart of brandy with a pound of honey, pour into the cask, and paste stiff brown paper over the bung-hole. Allow no hole for a vent peg, lest it should once be forgotten, and the whole cask of wine be spoiled. If the wine wants vent it will be sure to burst the paper; if not the paper will sufficiently exclude the air. Once a week or so it may be looked to; if the paper is burst, renew it, and continue to do so until it remains clear and dry.

A great difference of opinion prevails as to racking the wine, or suffering it to remain on the lees. Those who adopt the former plan do it at the end of six months; draw off the wine perfectly clear, and put it into a fresh cask, in which it is to remain six months, and then be bottled. If this plan is adopted, it may be better, instead of putting the brandy and honey in the first cask, to put it in that in which the wine is to be racked; but on the whole, it is, perhaps, preferable to leave the wine a year in the first cask, and then bottle it at once.

All British wines improve in the cask more than in the bottle. Have very nice clear and dry bottles; do not fill them too high. Good soft corks, made supple by soaking in a little of the wine; press them in, but do not knock. Keep the bottles lying in sawdust. This plan will apply equally well to raspberries, cherries, mulberries, and all kinds of ripe summer fruits.

COLORING FOR WINES

One pound of white sugar. Put into an iron kettle, let boil, and burn to a red black, and thick; remove from the fire, and add a little hot water, to keep it from hardening as it cools; then bottle for use.

FINING OR CLEARING

For fining or clearing the wine use one quarter pound of isinglass, dissolved in a portion of the wine, to a barrel. This must be put in after the fermentation is over, and should be added gently at the bung-hole, and managed so as to spread as much as possible over the upper surface of the liquid; the intention being that the isinglass should unite with impurities and carry them with it to the bottom.

TO FLAVOR WINE

When the vinous fermentation is about half-over, the flavoring ingredients are to be put into the vat and well stirred into the contents. If almonds form a component part, they are first to be beaten to a paste and mixed with a pint or two of the must. Nutmegs, cinnamon, ginger, seeds, etc., should, before they are put into the vat, be

17

reduced to powder, and mixed with some of the must.

TO MELLOW WINE

Wine, either in bottle or wood, will mellow much quicker when only covered with pieces of bladder well secured, than with corks or bungs. The bladder allows the watery particles to escape, but is impervious to alcohol.

TO REMOVE THE TASTE OF THE CASK FROM WINE

Finest oil of olives, one pound. Put it into the hogshead, bung close, and roll it about, or otherwise well agitate it, for three or four hours, then gib, and allow it to settle. The olive oil will gradually rise to the top and carry the ill flavor with it.

TO REMOVE ROPINESS FROM WINE

Add a little catechu or a small quantity of the bruised berries of the mountain ash.

TO RESTORE WINE WHEN SOUR OR SHARP

1. Fill a bag with leek-seed, or of leaves or twisters of vine, and put either of them to infuse in the cask.

2. Put a small quantity of powdered charcoal in the wine, shake it, and after it has remained still for forty-eight hours, decant steadily.

TO MAKE APPLE WINE

To every gallon of apple juice, immediately as it comes from the press, add two pounds of common loaf sugar; boil it as long as any scum rises, then strain it through a sieve, and let it cool. Add some good yeast, and stir it well. Let it work in the tub for two or three weeks, or till the head begins to flatten; then skim off the head, drain it clear off and tun it. When made a year, rack it off and fine it with isinglass; then add one-half pint of the best rectified spirit of wine or a pint of French brandy to every eight gallons.

APRICOCK WINE

Take three pounds of sugar, and three quarts of water; let them boil together and skim it well. Then put in six pounds of apricocks, pared and stoned, and let them boil until they are tender; then take them up and when the liquor is cold bottle it up. You may if you please, after you have taken out the apricocks, let the liquor have one

boil with a sprig of flowered clary in it;
the apricocks make marmalade, and are very
good for preserves.

BALM WINE

Take ten pounds of sugar, six quarts of
water, boil it gently for two hours; skim it
well and put it into a tub to cool. Take
three-quarters pound of the tops of balm,
bruise them, and put them into a barrel with
a little new yeast, and when the liquor is
cold, pour it on the balm. Stir it well together, and let it stand twenty-four hours,
stirring it often. Then close it up and let
it stand six weeks. Then rack it off and
put a lump of sugar into every bottle. Cork
it well, and it will be better the second year
than the first.

TO MAKE BARLEY WINE

Take one-half pound of French barley and
boil it in three waters, and save three pints
of the last water, and mix it with one quart
of white wine, one-half pint of borage water,
as much clary water, a little red rose-water,
the juice of five or six lemons, three-quarters
pound of fine sugar, the thin yellow rind of
a lemon. Brew all these quick together, run
it through a strainer, and bottle it up. It

is pleasant in hot weather, and very good
in fevers.

TO MAKE BEER AND ALE FROM PEA-SHELLS

Fill a boiler with green shells of peas, pour
on water till it rises half an inch above the
shells, and simmer for three hours. Strain
off the liquor, and add a strong decoction
of wood-sage, or hops, so as to render it
pleasantly bitter; ferment with yeast, and
bottle.

BIRCH WINE

The liquor of the birch-tree is to be obtained in the month of March, when the sap
begins to ascend. One foot from the ground
bore a hole in each tree, large enough to
admit a faucet, and set a vessel under; the
liquor will run for two or three days without
hurting the tree. Having obtained a sufficient quantity, stop the holes with pegs. To
each gallon of the liquor add one quart of
honey, or two and one-half pounds of sugar.
Boil together one hour, stirring it well. A
few cloves may be added for flavor, or the
rind of a lemon or two; and by all means
one ounce of hops to four and one-half gallons of wine.

Work it with yeast, tun, and refine with

isinglass. Two months after making, it may
be drawn off and bottled, and in two months
more will be fit for use, but will improve by
keeping.

BLACKBERRY WINE

Bruise the berries well with the hands. To
one gallon of fruit, add one-half gallon of
water, and let stand overnight. Strain and
measure, and to each gallon of juice add
two and one-half pounds of sugar. Put in
cask and let ferment. Tack thin muslin over
top, and when fermentation stops, pour into
jugs or kegs. Wine keeps best in kegs.

BLACKBERRY WINE
(OTHER METHODS OF MAKING)

1. Having procured berries that are fully
ripe, put them into a tub or pan with a tap
to it, and pour upon them as much boiling
water as will just cover them. As soon as
the heat will permit the hand to be put into
the vessel, bruise them well till all the berries are broken. Then let them stand covered
till the berries begin to rise toward the top,
which they usually do in three or four days.
Then draw off the clear liquor into another
vessel, and add to every ten quarts of this
liquor four pounds of sugar. Stir it well,

and let it stand to work a week or ten days; then filter it through a flannel jelly-bag into a cask. Take now four ounces of isinglass and lay it to steep for twelve hours in one pint of blackberry juice. The next morning boil it over a slow fire for one-half hour with one quart or three pints more juice, and pour it into the cask. When cool, rouse it well, and leave it to settle for a few days, then rack it off into a clean cask, and bung it down.

2. The following is said to be an excellent recipe for the manufacture of a superior wine from blackberries: Measure your berries, and bruise them; to every gallon, add one quart of boiling water. Let the mixture stand twenty-four hours, stirring occasionally; then strain off the liquor into a cask, to every gallon adding two pounds of sugar. Cork tight and let stand till the following October, and you will have wine ready for use, without any further straining or boiling, that will make lips smack, as they never smacked under similar influence before.

3. Gather when ripe, on a dry day. Put into a vessel, with the head out, and a tap fitted near the bottom; pour on them boiling water to cover them. Mash the berries with your hands, and let them stand covered till the pulp rises to the top and forms a

crust, in three or four days. Then draw off the fluid into another vessel, and to every gallon add one pound of sugar. Mix well, and put into a cask, to work for a week or ten days, and throw off any remaining lees, keeping the cask well filled, particularly at the commencement. When the working has ceased, bung it down; after six to twelve months, it may be bottled.

FINE BRANDY SHRUB

Take one ounce of citric acid, one pint of porter, one and one-half pints of raisin wine, one gill of orange-flower water, one gallon of good brandy, two and one-quarter quarts of water. First, dissolve the citric acid in the water, then add to it the brandy; next, mix the raisin wine, porter, and orange-flower water together; and lastly, mix the whole, and in a week or ten days it will be ready for drinking and of a very mellow flavor.

AMERICAN CHAMPAGNE

Seven quarts good cider (crab-apple cider is the best), one pint best fourth-proof brandy, one quart genuine champagne wine, one quart milk, one-half ounce of bitartrate of potassa. Mix and let stand a short time;

bottle while fermenting. An excellent imitation.

CHAMPAGNE CUP

To two ounces of powdered loaf sugar, put the juice and rind of one lemon pared thin; pour over these a large glass of dry sherry, and let it stand for an hour; then add one bottle of sparkling champagne and one bottle of soda water, a thin slice of fresh cucumber with the rind on, a sprig of borage or balm, and pour on blocks of clear ice.

BRITISH CHAMPAGNE

To every five pounds of rhubarb, when sliced and bruised, put one gallon of cold spring water. Let it stand three days, stirring two or three times every day; then press and strain it through a sieve, and to every gallon of liquor, put three and one-half pounds of loaf sugar. Stir it well, and when melted, barrel it. When it has done working, bung it up close, first suspending a muslin bag with isinglass from the bung into the barrel. To eight gallons of liquor, put two ounces of isinglass. In six months bottle it and wire the bottles; let them stand up for the first month, then lay four or five down lengthways for a week, and if none burst, all may be laid down. Should a large quantity be made, it must remain longer in cask. It may be colored pink by putting in a quart of raspberry juice. It will keep for many years.

BURGUNDY CHAMPAGNE

Fourteen pounds loaf sugar, twelve pounds brown sugar (pale), ten gallons warm water, one ounce white tartar. Mix, and at a proper temperature add one pint yeast. Afterwards, add one gallon sweet cider, two or three bitter almonds (bruised), one quart pale spirit, one-eighth ounce orris powder.

CHAMPAGNE CIDER

Champagne cider is made as follows: To five gallons of good cider put three pints of strained honey, or one and one-eighth pounds of good white sugar. Stir well and set it aside for a week. Clarify the cider with one-half gill of skimmed milk, or one teaspoonful of dissolved isinglass, and add one and one-half pints of pure spirits. After two or three days bottle the clear cider, and it will become sparkling. In order to produce a slow fermentation, the casks containing the fermenting liquor must be bunged up tight. It is a great object to retain

much of the carbonic gas in the cider, so
as to develop itself after being bottled.

CHAMPAGNE CIDER, NO. 2

One hogshead good pale vinous cider, three
gallons proof spirit (pale), fourteen pounds
honey or sugar. Mix, and let them remain
together in a temperate situation for one
month; then add one quart orange-flower
water, and fine it down with one-half gallon
skimmed milk. This will be very pale; and
a similar article, when bottled in champagne
bottles, silvered and labelled, has been often
sold to the ignorant for champagne. It
opens very brisk, if managed properly.

TO MAKE ENGLISH CHAMPAGNE, OR THE FINE CURRANT WINE

Take to three gallons of water nine pounds
of Lisbon sugar; boil the water and sugar
one-half hour, skim it clean. Then have one
gallon of currants picked, but not bruised.
Pour the liquor boiling hot over them, and
when cold, work it with one-half pint of balm
two days; then pour it through a flannel
or sieve; then put it into a barrel fit for
it, with one-half ounce of isinglass well
bruised. When it has done working, stop
it close for a month. Then bottle it, and in

27

every bottle put a very small lump of double refined sugar. This is excellent wine, and has a beautiful color.

SHAM CHAMPAGNE

One lemon sliced, one tablespoon tartaric acid, one ounce of race-ginger, one and one-half pounds sugar, two and one-half gallons of boiling water poured on the above. When blood warm, add one gill of distillery yeast, or two gills of home-brewed. Let it stand in the sun through the day. When cold, in the evening, bottle, cork, and wire it. In two days it is ready for use.

CHEAP AND AGREEABLE TABLE BEER

Take four and one-half gallons of water and boil one half, putting the other into a barrel; add the boiling water to the cold with one quart of molasses and a little yeast. Keep the bung-hole open until fermentation ceases.

CHERRY BOUNCE

Four quarts of wild cherries stemmed and well washed, four quarts of water. (I put mine in a big yellow bowl, and cover with double cheese-cloth, and set behind the kitchen stove for two weeks.) Skim every few days. Then strain, add three-quarters pound sugar to each quart of liquid, and let ferment again. This takes about two weeks. When it stops working, add rum, — about two bottles full for this quantity. (It is good without any rum.)

CHERRY BOUNCE, NO. 2

One quart of rum to one quart of wild cherries, and three-quarters pound of sugar. Put into a jug, and at first give it a frequent shake. Let it stand for several months before you pour off and bottle. A little water put on to the cherries left in the jug will make a pleasant and less ardent drink.

CHERRY BOUNCE, NO. 3

One gallon of good whiskey, one and one-half pints of wild black cherries bruised so as to break the stones, two ounces of common almonds shelled, two ounces of white sugar, one-half teaspoonful cinnamon, one-quarter teaspoonful cloves, one-quarter teaspoonful nutmeg, all bruised. Let stand twelve to thirteen days, and draw off. This, with the addition of one-half gallon of brandy, makes very nice cherry bounce.

TO MAKE CHERRY WINE

Pull off the stalks of the cherries, and mash them without breaking the stones; then press them hard through a hair bag, and to every gallon of liquor, put two pounds of sugar. The vessel must be full, and let it work as long as it makes a noise in the vessel; then stop it up close for a month or more, and when it is fine, draw it into dry bottles, and put a lump of sugar into every bottle. If it makes them fly, open them all for a moment, and then stop them up again. It will be fit to drink in a quarter of a year.

CHERRY WINE, NO. 2

Fifteen pounds of cherries, two pounds of currants. Bruise them together. Mix with them two-thirds of the kernels, and put the whole of the cherries, currants, and kernels into a barrel, with one-quarter pound of sugar to every pint of juice. The barrel must be quite full. Cover the barrel with vine leaves, and sand above them, and let it stand until it has done working, which will be in about three weeks; then stop it with a bung, and in two months' time it may be bottled.

2. Gather the cherries when quite ripe. Pull them from their stalks, and press them

through a hair sieve. To every gallon of the liquor add two pounds of lump sugar finely beaten; stir all together, and put it into a vessel that will just hold it. When it has done fermenting, stop it very close for three months, and then bottle it off for use.

GENERAL RULES FOR MAKING CIDER

Always choose perfectly ripe and sound fruit. Pick the apples by hand. (An active boy with the bag slung over his shoulder will soon clear a tree. Apples that have lain any time on the soil contract an earthy taste, which will always be found in the cider.)

After sweating, and before being ground, wipe them dry, and if any are found bruised or rotten, put them in a heap by themselves, for an inferior cider to make vinegar.

Always use hair cloths, instead of straw, to place between the layers of pomace. The straw when heated, gives a disagreeable taste to the cider.

As the cider runs from the press, let it pass through a hair sieve into a large open vessel that will hold as much juice as can be expressed in one day. In a day, or sometimes less, the pomace will rise to the top, and in a short time grow very thick. When little white bubbles break through it, draw off the liquor by a spigot, placed about three inches from the bottom, so that the lees may be left quietly behind.

The cider must be drawn off into very clean, sweet casks and closely watched. The moment the white bubbles before mentioned are perceived rising at the bung-hole, rack it again. When the fermentation is completely at an end, fill up the cask with cider, in all respects like that already contained in it, and bung it up tight, previous to which a tumbler of sweet oil may be poured into the bung-hole.

After being made and barrelled it should be allowed to ferment until it acquires the desired flavor, for perfectly sweet cider is not desirable. In the meantime clean barrels for its reception should be prepared thus: Some clean strips of rag are dipped into melted sulphur, lighted and hung in the bung-hole, and the bung laid loosely on the end of the rag. This is to allow the sulphur vapor to well fill the barrel. Tie up a half-pint of mustard-seed in a coarse muslin rag and put it into the barrel, then put your cider in. Now add the isinglass, which " fines " the cider but does not help to keep it sweet. This is the old-fashioned way, and

will keep cider in the same condition as it
went into the barrel, if kept in a cool place,
for a year. The sulphur vapor checks the
fermentation, and the sulphur in the mustard-seed keeps it checked. We hear that
professional cider dealers are now using the
bisulphite of lime instead of the mustard-
seed and the sulphur vapor. This bisulphite of lime is the same as the " preserving
powder." It is only another form of using
the sulphur, but it is more convenient and
perhaps more effectual. Another method is
to add sugar, one and a half pounds sugar
to a gallon of the cider, and let it ferment.
This makes a fermented, clear, good cider,
but sweet. It lasts sweet about six months,
if kept in a cool situation.

Preparatory to bottling cider it should
be examined, to see whether it be clear and
sparkling. If not, it should be clarified in
a similar way to beer, and left for a fortnight. The night before it is intended to
put it into bottles, the bung should be taken
out of the cask, and left so until the next
day, when it may be bottled, but not corked
down until the day after, as, if this be done
at once, many of the bottles will burst by
keeping. The best corks and champagne
bottles should be used, and it is usual to wire
and cover the corks with tinfoil, after the

manner of champagne. A few bottles may
be kept in a warm place to ripen, or a small
piece of lump sugar may be put into each
bottle before corking, if the cider be wanted
for immediate use, or for consumption during the cooler portion of the year, but for
warm weather and for long keeping this is
inadmissible. The bottled stock should be
stored in a cool cellar, when the quality
will be greatly improved by age.

TO CAN CIDER

Cider, if taken when first made, brought
to the boiling heat, and canned, precisely as
fruit is canned, will keep from year to year
without any change of taste. Canned up
this way in the fall, it may be kept a half-
dozen years or longer, as good as when first
made. It is better that the cider be settled
and poured off from the dregs, and when
brought to boiling heat the scum that gathers on the surface taken off; but the only
precaution necessary to preservation of the
cider is the sealing of it air tight when
boiling hot. The juice of other fruit can,
no doubt, be preserved in the same way. To
all tastes not already corrupted by strong
drinks, these unfermented juices are very

delicious. The juice of the grape is better than wine a century old, and more healthy. Churches believing in literal eating and drinking at the Lord's supper could in this way avoid the poisonous fermented spirits and drink the pure unfermented juice of the grape, as was doubtless done by the primitive Christians.

BOILING CIDER

To prepare cider for boiling, the first process is to filter it immediately on coming from the press. This is easiest done by placing some sticks crosswise in the bottom of a barrel, — a flour barrel with a single head is the best, — wherein an inch hole has been bored, and covering these sticks with say four inches of clean rye or wheat straw, and then filling the barrel to within a foot of the top with clean sand or coal dust, — sand is the best. Pour the cider as it comes from the press into the top of this barrel, drawing it off as soon as it comes out at the bottom into air-tight casks, and let it stand in the cellar until March. Then draw it out with as little exposure to the air as possible, put it into bottles that can be tightly and securely corked, and in two months it will be fit for use.

TO CLEAR CIDER

To clear and improve cider generally take two quarts of ground horseradish and one pound of thick gray filtering paper to the barrel, and either shake or stir until the paper has separated into small shreds, and let it stand for twenty-four hours, when the cider may be drawn off by means of a siphon or a stop cock. Instead of paper, a preparation of wool may be taken, which is to be had in the market, and which is preferable to paper, as it has simply to be washed with water, when it may be used again.

CIDER, TO PRESERVE AND KEEP SWEET

1. To one barrel of cider, put in one pound of mustard-seed, two pounds of raisins, one-quarter pound of the sticks (bark) of cinnamon. 2. When the cider in the barrel is in a lively fermentation, add as much white sugar as will be equal to one-quarter or three-quarters of a pound to each gallon of cider (according as the apples are sweet or sour); let the fermentation proceed until the liquid has the taste to suit, then add one-quarter of an ounce of sulphite (not sulphate) of lime to each gallon of cider, shake well, and let it stand three days, and

bottle for use. The sulphite should first be dissolved in a quart or so of cider before introducing it into the barrel of cider. 3. When fermentation commences in one barrel, draw off the liquor into another one, straining through a flannel cloth. Put into the cider three-quarters of an ounce of the oil of sassafras, and the same of the oil of wintergreen, well shaken up in a pint of alcohol. But one difficulty is said to pertain to this preparation of cider. It is so palatable that people won't keep it long.

CIDER CHAMPAGNE

Five gallons good cider, one quart spirit, one and one-quarter pounds honey or sugar. Mix, and let them rest for a fortnight, then fine with one gill of skimmed milk. This, put up in champagne bottles, silvered, and labelled, has often been sold for champagne. It opens very sparkling.

CHERRY CIDER

Seven gallons of apple cider, two quarts of dried black cherries, one pint of dried blueberries, one-half pint of elderberries, eighteen pounds of brown sugar.

DEVONSHIRE CIDER

The apples, after being plucked, are left in heaps in the orchard for some time, to complete their ripening, and render them more saccharine. They are then crushed between grooved cylinders, surmounted by a hopper, or in a circular trough, by two vertical edge-wheels of wood moved by a horse; after passing through which, they are received into large tubs or crocks, and are then called pomace. They are afterwards laid on the vat in alternate layers of the pomace and clean straw, called reeds. They are then pressed, a little water being occasionally added. The juice passes through a hair sieve, or similar strainer, and is received in a large vessel, whence it is run into casks or open vats, where everything held in mechanical suspension is deposited. The fermentation is often slow of being developed; though the juice be set in November or December, the working sometimes hardly commences till March. Till this time the cider is sweet; it now becomes pungent and vinous, and is ready to be racked for use. If the fermentation continue, it is usual to rack it again into a clean cask that has been well sulphured out, and to leave behind the head and sediment; or two or three cans of cider are put into a clean cask, and a match of brimstone burned in it. It is then agitated, by which the fermentation of that quantity is completely stopped. The cask is then nearly filled, the fermentation of the whole is checked, the process of racking is repeated until it becomes so, and is continued from time to time till the cider is in a quiet state and fit for drinking.

FRENCH CIDER

After the fruit is mashed in a mill, between iron cylinders, it is allowed to remain in a large tun or tub for fourteen or fifteen hours, before pressing. The juice is placed in casks, which are kept quite full, and so placed under gawntrees, or stillions, that small tubs may be put under them, to receive the matter that works over. At the end of three or four days for sweet cider, and nine or ten days for strong cider, it is racked into sulphured casks, and then stored in a cool place.

WESTERN CIDER

To one pound of sugar, add one-half ounce of tartaric acid, two tablespoonfuls of good yeast. Dissolve the sugar in one quart of warm water; put all in a gallon jug, shake it well, fill the jug with pure cold water, let it stand uncorked twelve hours, and it is fit for use.

CIDER WITHOUT APPLES

To each gallon of cold water, put one pound common sugar, one-half ounce tartaric acid, one tablespoonful of yeast. Shake well, make in the evening, and it will be fit for use next day. Make in a keg a few gallons at a time, leaving a few quarts to make into next time, not using yeast again until keg needs rinsing. If it gets a little sour, make a little more into it, or put as much water with it as there is cider, and put it with the vinegar. If it is desired to bottle this cider by manufacturers of small drinks, you will proceed as follows: five gallons hot water, thirty pounds brown sugar, three-quarters pound tartaric acid, twenty-five gallons cold water, three pints of hops or brewers' yeast worked into paste with three-quarters pound flour, and one pint water will be required in making this paste. Put all together in a barrel, which it will fill, and let it work twenty-four hours, the yeast running out at a bung all the time, by putting in a little occasionally to keep it full. Then bottle, putting in two or three broken raisins to each bottle, and it will nearly equal champagne.

CIDER WINE

Let the new cider from sour apples (ripe, sound fruit preferred) ferment from one to three weeks, as the weather is warm or cool. When it has attained to a lively fermentation, add to each gallon, according to its acidity, from one-half pound to two pounds of white crushed sugar, and let the whole ferment until it possesses precisely the taste which it is desired should be permanent. In this condition pour out one quart of the cider, and add for each gallon of cider one-quarter ounce of sulphite of lime, not sulphate. Stir the powder and cider until intimately mixed, and return the emulsion to the fermenting liquid. Agitate briskly and thoroughly for a few moments, and then let the cider settle. Fermentation will cease at once. When, after a few days, the cider has become clear, draw off carefully, to avoid the sediment, and bottle. If loosely corked, which is better, it will become a sparkling cider wine, and may be kept indefinitely long.

TO MAKE CLARY WINE

Take twelve pounds of Malaga raisins, pick them and chop them very small, put them in a tub, and to each pound one-half pint of water. Let them steep ten or eleven

41

days, stirring it twice every day; you must keep it covered close all the while. Then strain it off, and put it into a vessel, and about one-quarter peck of the tops of clary, when it is in blossom; stop it close for six weeks, and then bottle it off. In two or three months it is fit to drink. It is apt to have a great sediment at bottom; therefore it is best to draw it off by plugs, or tap it pretty high.

TO MAKE FINE CLARY WINE

To five gallons of water put twelve and one-half pounds of sugar, and the whites of six eggs well beaten. Set it over the fire, and let it boil gently near an hour; skim it clean and put it in a tub, and when it is near cold, then put into the vessel you keep it in about half a strike of clary in the blossom, stripped from the stalks, flowers and little leaves together, and one pint of new ale-yeast. Then put in the liquor, and stir it two or three times a day for three days; when it has done working, stop it up, and bottle it at three or four months old, if it is clear.

CLOVER WINE

Three quarts blossoms, four quarts boiling water; let stand three days. Drain, and to the flower heads add three more quarts of water and the peel of one lemon. Boil fifteen minutes, drain, and add to other juice. To every quart, add one pound of sugar; ferment with one cup of yeast. Keep in warm room three weeks, then bottle.

TO MAKE COCK ALE

Take five gallons of ale, and a large cock, the older the better. Parboil the cock, flay him, and stamp him in a stone mortar till his bones are broken (you must craw and gut him when you flay him), then put the cock into one quart of sack, and put to it one and one-half pounds of raisins of the sun stoned, some blades of mace, and a few cloves. Put all these into a canvas bag, and a little before you find the ale has done working, put the ale and bag together into a vessel. In a week or nine days' time bottle it up; fill the bottle but just above the neck, and give it the same time to ripen as other ale.

TO MAKE COWSLIP WINE

To three gallons of water put seven pounds of sugar; stir it well together, and beat the whites of ten eggs very well, and mix with the liquor, and make it boil as fast as possible. Skim it well, and let it continue boiling two hours; then strain it through a hair sieve, and set it a cooling, and when it is cold as wort should be, put a small quantity of yeast to it on a toast, or in a dish. Let it stand all night working; then bruise one-half peck of cowslips, put them into your vessel, and your liquor upon them, adding three ounces of syrup of lemons. Cut a turf of grass and lay on the bung; let it stand a fortnight, and then bottle it. Put your tap into your vessel before you put your wine in, that you may not shake it.

COWSLIP OR CLARY WINE, NO. 2

The best method of making these wines is to put in the pips dry, when the fermentation of the wine has subsided. This method is preferred for two reasons: first, it may be performed at any time of the year when lemons are cheapest, and when other wine is making; second, all waste of the pips is avoided. Being light, they are sure to work over if put in the cask while the wine is in a state of fermentation. Boil fourteen pounds of good moist sugar with five gallons of water, and one ounce of hops. Shave thin the rinds of eight lemons or Seville oranges, or part of each; they must be put in the boil the last quarter of an hour, or

the boiling liquor poured over them.
Squeeze the juice to be added when cool, and
rinse the pulp in the hot liquor, and keep
it filled up, either with wine or new beer, as
long as it works over; then paste brown
paper, and leave it for four, six, or eight
months. The quantity of flowers is one
quart of flowers to each gallon of wine.
Let them be gathered on a fine, dry day, and
carefully picked from every bit of stalk and
green. Spread them thinly on trays, sheets,
or papers, and turn them often. When
thoroughly dry put them in paper bags,
until the wine is ready to receive them. Put
them in at the bung-hole; stir them down
two or three times a day, till all the cowslips
have sunk; at the same time add isinglass.
Then paste over again with paper. In six
months the wine will be fit to bottle, but will
be improved by keeping longer in the cask.
The pips shrink into a very small compass
in drying; the quantity allowed is of fresh-
gathered flowers. Observe, also, that wine
well boiled, and refined with hops and isinglass, is just as good used from the cask
as if bottled, which is a great saving of time
and hazard. Wine made on the above prin-
ciples has been often praised by connois-
seurs, and supposed to have been bottled
half a day.

CURRANT SHRUB

Take white currants when quite ripe, pick them off the stalks, and bruise them. Strain out the juice through a cloth, and to two quarts of the juice put two pounds of loaf sugar; when it is dissolved, add one gallon of rum, then strain through a flannel bag that will keep in the jelly, and it will run off clear. Then bottle for use.

CURRANT WINE

Take four gallons of currants, not too ripe, and strip them into an earthen stein that has a cover to it. Then take two and one-half gallons of water and five and one-half pounds of double refined sugar; boil the sugar and water together, skim it, and pour it boiling hot on the currants, letting it stand forty-eight hours; then strain it through a flannel bag into the stein again, let it stand a fortnight to settle, and bottle it out.

CURRANT WINE, NO. 2

The currants should be fully ripe when picked. Put them into a large tub, in which they should remain a day or two, then crush with the hands, unless you have a small patent wine-press, in which they should not

be pressed too much, or the stems will be
bruised, and impart a disagreeable taste to
the juice. If the hands are used, put the
crushed fruit, after the juice has been
poured off, in a cloth or sack and press out
the remaining juice. Put the juice back
into the tub after cleansing it, where it
should remain about three days, until the
first stages of fermentation are over, and
remove once or twice a day the scum copi-
ously arising to the top. Then put the juice
in a vessel, — a demijohn, keg, or barrel,
— of a size to suit the quantity made, and
to each quart of juice add three pounds of
the best yellow sugar, and soft water sufficient to make a gallon. Thus, ten quarts
of juice and thirty pounds of sugar will give
you ten gallons of wine, and so on in proportion. Those who do not like sweet wine
can reduce the quantity of sugar to two and
one-half, or who wish it very sweet, raise
to three and one-half pounds per gallon.
The vessel must be full, and the bung or
stopper left off until fermentation ceases,
which will be in twelve or fifteen days.
Meanwhile, the cask must be filled up daily
with currant juice left over, as fermentation
throws out the impure matter. When fermentation ceases, rack the wine off carefully,
either from the spigot or by a siphon, and

keep running all the time. Cleanse the cask
thoroughly with boiling water, then return
the wine, bung up tightly, and let it stand
four or five months, when it will be fit to drip,
and can be bottled if desired. All the ves-
sels, casks, etc., should be perfectly sweet,
and the whole operation should be done with
an eye to cleanliness. In such event, every
drop of brandy or other spirituous liquors
added will detract from the flavor of the
wine, and will not in the least degree increase
its keeping qualities. Currant wine made in
this way will keep for an age.

CURRANT WINE, NO. 3

To every pailful of currants, on the stem,
put one pailful of water; mash and strain.
To each gallon of the mixture of juice and
water add three and one-quarter pounds of
sugar. Mix well and put into your cask,
which should be placed in the cellar, on the
tilt, that it may be racked off in October,
without stirring up the sediment. Two
bushels of currants will make one barrel of
wine. Four gallons of the mixture of juice
and water will, after thirteen pounds of
sugar are added, make five gallons of wine.
The barrel should be filled within three inches
of the bung, which must be made air tight

by placing wet clay over it after it is driven in.

2. Pick your currants when ripe on a fair day, crush them well, and to every gallon of juice add two gallons of water and three pounds of sugar; if you wish it sweeter, add another one-half pound of sugar. Mix all together in some large vessel, then dip out into earthen jars. Let it stand to ferment in some cool place, skimming it every other morning. In about ten days it will be ready to strain off; bottle and seal, or put in a cask and cork tight. The longer you keep it the better it will be.

CURRANT WINE, NO. 4

Into a five gallon keg put five quarts of currant juice, fifteen pounds of sugar, and fill up with water. Let it stand in a cool place until sufficiently worked, and then bung up tight. You can let it remain in the cask, and draw out as you want to use it.

CURRANT OR GOOSEBERRY WINE, WITHOUT BOILING

Take ten quarts of fruit, bruise it, and add to it five quarts of water. Stir it well together, and let it stand twelve hours; then strain it through a coarse canvas bag or hair sieve, add eleven pounds of good Lisbon sugar, and stir it well. Put the pulp of the fruit into a gallon more water; stir it about and let it stand twelve hours. Then strain to the above, again stirring it; cover the tub with a sack. In a day or two the wine will begin to ferment. When the whole surface is covered with a thick, yeasty froth, begin to skim it on to a sieve. What runs through may be returned to the wine. Do this from time to time for several days, till no more yeast forms. Then put it into the cask.

IMITATION OF CYPRESS WINE

To five gallons of water put five quarts of the juice of white elderberries, pressed gently through a sieve without bruising the seeds. Add to every gallon of liquor one and one-half pounds of sugar, and to the whole quantity one ounce of sliced ginger, and one-half ounce of cloves. Boil this nearly an hour, taking off the scum as it rises, and pour in an open tub to cool. Work it with ale yeast spread upon a toast of bread for three days. Then turn it into a vessel that will just hold it, adding about three-quarters pound bruised raisins, to lie in the liquor till drawn off, which should not be done till the wine is fine.

DAISY WINE

One quart of daisy heads, one quart of cold water. Let stand forty-eight hours. Strain and add three-quarters pound of sugar to each quart of liquid. Let stand about two weeks, or till it stops fermenting. Strain again and bottle. It improves with keeping.

DANDELION WINE

Four quarts of dandelions. Cover with four quarts of boiling water; let stand three days. Add peel of three oranges and one lemon. Boil fifteen minutes; drain and add juice of oranges and lemon to four pounds of sugar and one cup of yeast. Keep in warm room and strain again; let stand for three weeks. It is then ready to bottle and serve.

DAMSON WINE

Gather the fruit dry, weigh, and bruise it, and to every eight pounds of fruit add one gallon of water; boil the water, pour it on the fruit scalding hot. Let it stand for two days; then draw it off, put it into a clean cask, and to every gallon of liquor add two and one-half pounds of good sugar. Fill the cask. It may be bottled off after standing in the cask a year. On bottling

the wine, put a small lump of loaf sugar
into every bottle.

DAMSON, OR BLACK CHERRY WINE

Damson, or Black Cherry Wine may be
made in the same manner, excepting the addition of spice, and that the sugar should
be finer. If kept in an open vessel four days,
these wines will ferment of themselves; but
it is better to forward the process by the use
of a little yeast, as in former recipes. They
will be fit for use in about eight months. As
there is a flatness belonging to both these
wines if bottled, a teaspoonful of rice, a
lump or two of sugar, or four or five raisins
will tend to enliven it.

EBULUM

To one hogshead of strong ale take a
heaped bushel of elderberries, and one-half
pound of juniper-berries beaten. Put in all
the berries when you put in the hops, and
let them boil together till the berries break
in pieces, then work it up as you do ale.
When it has done working add to it one-half
pound of ginger, one-half ounce of cloves,
one-half ounce of mace, one ounce of nutmegs, one ounce of cinnamon, grossly
beaten, one-half pound of citron, one-half

pound of eringo root, and likewise of candied orange-peel. Let the sweetmeats be cut in pieces very thin, and put with the spice into a bag, and hang it in the vessel when you stop it up. So let it stand till it is fine, then bottle it up, and drink it with lumps of double refined sugar in the glass.

ELDER - FLOWER WINE

Take the flowers of elder, and be careful that you don't let any stalks in; to every quart of flowers put one gallon of water, and three pounds of loaf sugar. Boil the water and sugar a quarter of an hour, then pour it on the flowers and let it work three days; then strain the wine through a hair sieve, and put it into a cask. To every ten gallons of wine add one ounce of isinglass dissolved in cider, and six whole eggs. Close it up and let it stand six months, and then bottle it.

TO MAKE ELDER WINE

Take five pounds of Malaga raisins, rub them and shred them small; then take one gallon of water, boil it an hour, and let it stand till it is but blood-warm; then put it in an earthen crock or tub, with your raisins. Let them steep ten days, stirring them once or twice a day; then pass the liquor through a hair sieve, and have in readiness one pint of the juice of elderberries drawn off as you do for jelly of currants; then mix it cold with the liquor, stir it well together, put it into a vessel, and let it stand in a warm place. When it has done working, stop it close. Bottle it about Candlemas.

ELDERBERRY WINE

Nine quarts elderberry juice, nine quarts water, eleven and one-half pounds white sugar, two ounces red tartar. These are put into a cask, a little yeast added, and the whole is fermented. When undergoing fermentation, one ounce ginger root, one ounce allspice, one-quarter ounce cloves are put into a bag of clean cotton cloth, and suspended in the cask. They will give a pleasant flavor to the wine, which will become clear in about two months, and may be drawn off and bottled. Add some brandy to this wine, but if the fermentation is properly conducted, this is not necessary.

ELDER WINE, NO. 2

Take spring-water, and let it boil half an hour; then measure two and one-half gallons, and let it stand to cool. Then have in

readiness ten pounds of raisins of the sun
well picked and rubbed in a cloth, and hack
them so as to cut them, but not too small;
then put them in, the water being cold, and
let them stand nine days, stirring them two
or three times a day. Then have ready
three pints of the juice of elderberries full
ripe, which must be infused in boiling water,
or baked three hours; then strain out the
raisins, and when the elder liquor is cold,
mix that with it, but it is best to boil up the
juice to a syrup, one-half pound of sugar
to every pint of juice. Boil and skim it,
and when cold mix it with your raisin liquor,
and two or three spoonfuls of good ale yeast.
Stir it well together; then put it into a
vessel fit for it, let it stand in a warm place
to work, and in your cellar five or six
months.

ELDER WINE, NO. 3

The quantity of fruit required is one gallon of ripe elderberries, and one quart of
damsons or sloes, for every two gallons of
wine to be produced. Boil them in water
till the damsons burst, frequently breaking
them with a flat stick; then strain and return the liquor to the copper. The quantity of liquor required for nine gallons of

wine will be ten gallons; therefore if the
first liquor proves short of this, add water
to the pulp, rub it about and strain to the
rest. Boil two hours with twenty-three
pounds of coarse moist sugar; three-quarters of a pound of ginger bruised, one-half
a pound of allspice, and one ounce of cinnamon, loosely tied in a muslin bag, and two
or three ounces of hops. When quite cool
work on the foregoing plan, tun in two days,
drop in the spice, and suspend the bag by
a string not long enough to let it touch the
bottom of the cask; fill it up for a fortnight, then paste over stiff brown paper.
It will be fit to tap in two months; will keep
for years, but does not improve by age like
many other wines. It is never better than
in the first year of its age.

ELDER WINE (FLAVORED WITH HOPS)

The berries, which must be thoroughly
ripe, are to be stripped from the stalk, and
squeezed to a pulp. Stir and squeeze this
pulp every day for four days; then separate the juice from the pulp by passing
through a cane sieve or basket. To every
gallon of juice, add one-half gallon of cold
water. Boil four and one-half gallons with

three ounces of hops for one-half hour; then strain it and boil again, with one and one-half pounds of sugar to the gallon, for about ten minutes, skimming all the time; pour it into a cooler, and, while luke-warm, put a piece of bread with a little balm on it to set it working. Put it into a cask as soon as cold; when it has done working, cork it down, and leave it six months before it is tapped. It is then drinkable, but improves with age exceedingly.

TO MAKE ELDER WINE AT CHRISTMAS

Take five pounds of Malaga or Lipara raisins, rub them clean, and shred them small. Then take five quarts of water, boil it an hour, and when it is near cold put it in a tub with the raisins; let them steep ten days, and stir them once or twice a day. Then strain it through a hair sieve, and by infusion draw one pint of elder-juice, and one-quarter of a pint of damson juice. Make the juice into a thin syrup, a pound of sugar to a pint of juice, and not boil it much, but just enough to keep. When you have strained out the raisin liquor, put that and the syrup into a vessel fit for it, and one-half a pound of sugar. Stop the bung

with a cork till it gathers to a head, then
open it, and let it stand till it has done
working; then put the cork in again, and
stop it very close, and let it stand in a warm
place two or three months, and then bottle
it. Make the elder and damson juice into
syrup in its season, and keep it in a cool
cellar till you have convenience to make the
wine.

TO MAKE ELDER - FLOWER WATER

Take two large handfuls of dried elder-
flowers, and ten gallons of spring-water;
boil the water, and pour it scalding hot upon
the flowers. The next day put to every
gallon of water five pounds of Malaga raisins, the stalks being first picked off, but not
washed; chop them grossly with a chop-
ping-knife, then put them into your boiled
water, and stir the water, raisins, and flowers well together, and so do twice a day for
twelve days. Then press out the juice clear,
as long as you can get any liquor out.
Then put it in your barrel fit for it, and
stop it up two or three days till it works,
and in a few days stop it up close, and let
it stand two or three months, till it is clear;
then bottle it.

ENGLISH FIG WINE

Take the large blue figs when pretty ripe, and steep them in white wine, having made some slits in them, that they may swell and gather in the substance of the wine. Then slice some other figs and let them simmer over a fire in water until they are reduced to a kind of pulp. Then strain out the water, pressing the pulp hard and pour it as hot as possible on the figs that are imbrued in the wine. Let the quantities be nearly equal, but the water somewhat more than the wine and figs. Let them stand twenty-four hours, mash them well together, and draw off what will run without squeezing. Then press the rest, and if not sweet enough add a sufficient quantity of sugar to make it so. Let it ferment, and add to it a little honey and sugar candy, then fine it with white of eggs, and a little isinglass, and draw it off for use.

TO MAKE FRONTIGNAC WINE

Take three gallons of water, six pounds of white sugar, and three pounds of raisins of the sun cut small; boil these together an hour. Then take of the flowers of elder, when they are falling, and will shake off, the quantity of half a peck; put them in the liquor when it is almost cold. The next day

put in three spoonfuls of syrup of lemons
and two spoonfuls of ale-yeast, and two days
after put it in a vessel that is fit for it, and
when it has stood two months, bottle it off.

GINGER BEER

The proportions of this may vary. Loaf
sugar is preferable to moist; some say a
pound to a gallon, others a pound and a half.
Some allow but half an ounce of ginger
(sliced or bruised) to a gallon, others an
ounce. A lemon to a gallon is the usual proportion, to which some add a quarter of an
ounce or half an ounce of cream of tartar.
The white of an egg to each gallon is useful for clarifying, but not absolutely necessary. Some people put a quarter of a pint
of brandy to four gallons of beer by way of
keeping it; half an ounce of hops boiled in
it would answer the same purpose. Boil the
sugar, and shaved rind of lemons; let it
boil half an hour. Clear the lemons of the
white pith and put them in the wine. When
cool, stir in the yeast (two tablespoonfuls to
a gallon), put it in the barrel without straining, and bung close. In a fortnight draw
off and bottle. It will be ready for use in
another fortnight, and will keep longer than
ginger pop. If cream of tartar is used, pour
the boiling liquor over it, but do not boil it.

GINGER BEER, NO. 2

Seven pounds crushed white sugar, eight gallons water, one-half cup of yeast, four ounces best powdered ginger, a few drops of essence of lemon, one-half teaspoonful essence of cloves. To the ginger pour one pint of boiling water and let it stand fifteen or twenty minutes. Dissolve the sugar in two quarts of warm water, pour both into a barrel half-filled with cold water, then add the essence and the yeast; let it stand one-half hour, then fill up with cold water. Let it ferment six to twelve hours and bottle.

GINGER WINE

Take four gallons of water, ten pounds of loaf sugar, one and one-quarter pounds of bruised ginger, one ounce of hops, the shaved rinds of five lemons or Seville oranges. Let these boil together for two hours, carefully skimming. Pour it, without straining, on to two pounds of raisins. When cool, put in the juice of the lemons or oranges; rinse the pulp in a pint or two of the wine, and strain it to the rest. Ferment it with yeast; mix one-half cup of solid yeast with a pint or two of the wine, and with that work the rest. Next day tun it, raisins, hops, ginger, and all together, and fill it up for a fortnight either with wine or with good new beer; then dissolve one ounce of isinglass in a little of the wine, and return it to the rest to fine it. A few days afterward bung it close.

This wine will be in full perfection in six months. It may be bottled, but is apt to fly; and if made exactly by the above directions, and drawn from the cask, it will sparkle like champagne.

TO MAKE GOOSEBERRY WINE

Boil four gallons of water, and one-half pound of sugar an hour, skim it well, and let it stand till it is cold. Then to every quart of that water, allow one and one-half pounds of gooseberries, first beaten or bruised very well; let it stand twenty-four hours. Then strain it out, and to every gallon of this liquor put three pounds of sugar; let it stand in the vat twelve hours. Then take the thick scum off, and put the clear into a vessel fit for it, and let it stand a month; then draw it off, and rinse the vessel with some of the liquor. Put it in again, and let it stand four months, and bottle it.

GOOSEBERRY WINE

Take to every four pounds of gooseberries one and one-quarter pounds of sugar, and one quart of fair water. Bruise the berries, and steep them twenty-four hours in the water, stirring them often; then press the liquor from them, and put your sugar to the liquor. Then put in a vessel fit for it, and when it is done working stop it up, and let it stand a month; then rack it off into another vessel, and let it stand five or six weeks longer. Then bottle it out, putting a small lump of sugar into every bottle; cork your bottles well, and three months' end it will be fit to drink. In the same manner is currant and raspberry wine made; but cherry wine differs, for the cherries are not to be bruised, but stoned, and put the sugar and water together, and give it a boil and a skim, and then put in your fruit, letting it stew with a gentle fire a quarter of an hour, and then let it run through a sieve without pressing, and when it is cold put it in a vessel, and order it as your gooseberry or currant wine. The only cherries for wine are the great bearers, Murray cherries, Morelloes, Black Flanders, or the John Treduskin cherries.

GOOSEBERRY WINE, NO. 2

Pick and bruise the gooseberries, and to every pound of berries put one quart of cold spring water, and let it stand three

days, stirring it twice or thrice a day. Add
to every gallon of juice three pounds of loaf
sugar. Fill the barrel, and when it is done
working, add to every ten quarts of liquor
one pint of brandy and a little isinglass.
The gooseberries must be picked when they
are just changing color. The liquor ought
to stand in the barrel six months. Taste it
occasionally, and bottle when the sweetness
has gone off.

GOOSEBERRY AND CURRANT WINE

The following method of making superior
gooseberry and currant wines is recom-
mended in a French work.

For currant wine four pounds of honey,
dissolved in seven gallons of boiling water,
to which, when clarified, is added the juice
of four pounds of red or white currants.
It is then fermented for twenty-four hours
and one pound of sugar to every one gallon
of water is added. The preparation is
afterward clarified with whites of eggs and
cream of tartar.

For gooseberry wine, the fruit is gathered dry when about half-ripe, and then
pounded in a mortar. The juice when properly strained is mixed with sugar in the
proportion of three pounds to every two

gallons of juice. It is then left in a quiet state for fifteen days, at the expiration of which it is carefully poured off and left to ferment for three months, when the quantity is under fifteen gallons, and five months when double that quantity. It is then bottled and soon becomes fit for drinking.

PEARL GOOSEBERRY WINE

Take as many as you please of the best gooseberries, bruise them, and let them stand all night. The next morning press or squeeze them out and let the liquor stand to settle seven or eight hours; then pour off the clear from the settling, and measure it as you put it into your vessel, adding to every three pints of liquor one pound of double refined sugar. Break your sugar into fine lumps, and put it in the vessel with a bit of isinglass, stop it up, and at three months' end bottle it out, putting into every bottle a lump of double refined sugar. This is the fine gooseberry wine.

RED GOOSEBERRY WINE

Take five gallons cold soft water, five and one-half gallons red gooseberries, and ferment. Now mix eight pounds raw sugar, one pound beet root sliced, one-half ounce red tartar in fine powder. Afterward put in one-balf pound sassafras chips, one-half gallon brandy or less. This will make nine gallons.

RED AND WHITE GOOSEBERRY WINE

Take one and one-half gallons cold soft water, three quarts red gooseberries, two quarts white gooseberries. Ferment. Now mix two and one-half pounds raw sugar, three-quarters pound honey, one-half ounce tartar in fine powder. Afterwards put in one ounce bitter almonds, a small handful sweet briar, two quarts brandy or less.

WHITE GOOSEBERRY OR CHAM-PAGNE WINE

Take four and one-half gallons cold soft water and fifteen quarts of white goose-berries. Ferment. Now mix six pounds re-fined sugar, four pounds honey, one ounce white tartar in fine powder. Put in one ounce dry orange and lemon peel, or two ounces fresh, and add one-half gallon white brandy. This will make nine gallons.

UNFERMENTED GRAPE JUICE

Wash and take from the stems ten pounds ripe Concord grapes. Add two quarts water and bring them to a boil. Use a potato masher. When the seeds separate, strain through double cheese-cloth. Add two pounds of granulated sugar and strain again. Bring again to a boil and bottle directly, boiling hot, cork and seal, or put into patent bottles. Serve with cracked ice in the glass or diluted with about one-third ice water.

GRAPE WINE

Two quarts of grape juice, two quarts of water, four pounds of sugar. Extract the juice of the grape in any simple way; if only a few quarts are desired, we do it with a strainer and a pair of squeezers; if a large quantity is desired, put the grapes into a cheese-press made particularly clean, putting on sufficient weight to extract the juice of a full hoop of grapes, being careful that none but perfect grapes are used, perfectly ripe and free from blemish. After the first pressing, put a little water with the pulp and press a second time, using the juice of the second pressing with the water to be mixed with the clear grape juice. If only a few quarts are made, place the wine as soon as mixed into bottles, filling them even full, and allow to stand in a warm place until it ferments, which will take about thirty-six hours usually; then remove all the scum, cool, and put into a dark, cool place. If a few gallons are desired, place in a keg, but the keg must be even full, and after fermentation has taken place and the scum removed, draw off and bottle, and cork tight.

GRAPE WINE, NO. 2

The larger the proportion of juice and the less of water, the nearer it will approach to the strength and richness of foreign wine. There ought not to be less than one-third juice pure. Squeeze the grapes in a hair sieve, bruising them with the hand rather than any heavier press, as it is better not to crush the stones. Soak the pulp in water until a sufficient quantity is obtained to fill up the cask. As loaf sugar is to be used for this wine, and it is not easily dissolved in cold liquid, the best plan is to pour over the sugar, three pounds in every gallon required, as much boiling water as will dissolve it, and stir till it is dissolved. When cold, put it in the cask with the juice, fill up from water in which the pulp has been steeped. To each gallon of wine, put one-half ounce of bitter almonds, not blanched, but cut small.

The fermentation will not be very great. When it subsides, proceed with brandy and papering.

GRAPE WINE, NO. 3

Crush the grapes and let them stand one week. Drain off the juice, strain; add one quart of water and three pounds of sugar to each gallon. Put in a barrel or cask with a thin piece of muslin tacked over the bung-hole, and let stand until fermentation stops. Put in a cask and seal securely, and let stand six months. Then bottle and seal and keep in cool place.

HOP BEER

Turn five quarts of water on six ounces of hops; boil three hours. Strain off the liquor; turn on four quarts more of water, and twelve spoonfuls of ginger, and boil the hops three hours longer. Strain and mix it with the other liquor, and stir in two quarts of molasses. Brown, very dry, one-half pound of bread, and put in, — rusked bread is best. Pound it fine, and brown it in a pot, like coffee. After cooling to be about luke-warm, add one pint of new yeast that is free from salt. Keep the beer covered, in a temperate situation, till fermentation has ceased, which is known by the settling of the froth; then turn it into a keg or bottles, and keep it in a cool place.

JUNIPER-BERRY WINE

Take four and one-half gallons of cold soft water, seven pounds Malaga or Smyrna raisins, two and one-quarter quarts juniper-berries, one-half ounce red tartar, one-half handful wormwood, one-half handful sweet marjoram, one pint whiskey or more. Ferment for ten or twelve days.

KOUMISS, A TARTAR WINE

Take a quantity of fresh mare's milk, add to it one-sixth part water, pour the mixture into a wooden bowl. Use as a ferment one-eighth part of skimmed milk; but at any future preparation, a small portion of old koumiss will answer better. Cover the vessel with a thick cloth and set in a moderately warm place for twenty-four hours, at the end of which time the milk will have become sour, and a thick substance gathered at the top. Now, with a churn-staff, beat it till the thick substance above mentioned be blended intimately with the adjacent fluid. Leave it to rest twenty-four hours more; after which pour it into a higher and narrower vessel resembling a churn, where the agitation must be repeated as before. In this state it is called koumiss. The taste should be a pleasant mixture of sweet and sour. It should always be well shaken before used.

KOUMISS

Heat four cups milk; cool; when lukewarm, add one-fourth yeast cake dissolved in one-fourth cup lukewarm water, and two tablespoons sugar. Pour into bottles with patent stoppers, fill two-thirds full, cork tightly. Shake; let stand in kitchen six hours, then on ice for twenty-four hours; serve ice cold.

TO MAKE LEMON WINE

Take six large lemons, pare off the rind, and squeeze out the juice; steep the rind in the juice, and put to it one quart of brandy. Let it stand in an earthen pot close stopped three days, then squeeze six more, and mix with two quarts of water, and as much sugar as will sweeten the whole. Boil the water, lemons, and sugar together, letting it stand till it is cool; then add one quart of white wine, and the other lemon and brandy, and mix them together, and run it through a flannel bag into some vessel. Let it stand three months and bottle it off; cork your bottles very well, and keep it cool. It will be fit to drink in a month or six weeks.

LEMON WINE, NO. 2

Four pounds sugar, one pound raisins (bruised), two gallons water. Boil, then add one gallon cider. Ferment, and add one quart of spirits, three-quarters ounce white tartar, a few drops essence of lemon. Observe to shake the essence, with a little of the spirit, until it becomes milky, before adding it to the wine.

MADEIRA WINE

To five gallons prepared cider, add one-half ounce tartaric acid, one-half pint spirits, one-half pound loaf sugar. Let it stand ten days, draw it off carefully, fine it down, and again rack it into another cask.

MALT WINE, OR ENGLISH SHERRY

Take twelve pounds of good moist sugar, two gallons of water. Boil them together two hours, skimming carefully. When the scum is all removed, and the liquor looks clear, add one-half ounce of hops, which should boil one-quarter hour or twenty minutes. When the liquor is quite cold, add to it five quarts of strong beer in the height of working; cover up and let it work forty-eight hours; then skim and tun. If none remains for filling up, use new beer for that purpose. This method may be adopted with all boiled wines, and will be found to improve their strength and promote their keeping. In a fortnight or three weeks, when the head begins to sink, add two and one-half pounds raisins (free from stalks), one ounce of sugar candy, one ounce of bitter almonds, one-half cup of the best brandy; brown paper, as in former articles. It may be bottled in one year; but if left three years in the wood, and then bottled, it will be found equal in strength and flavor to foreign wine.

MEAD

The following is a good recipe for mead: On five pounds of honey pour five quarts of boiling water; boil, and remove the scum as it rises; add one-quarter ounce of best hops, and boil for ten minutes. Then pour the liquor into a tub to cool; when all but cold, add a little yeast spread upon a slice of toasted bread. Let it stand in a warm room. When fermentation is finished, bung it down, leaving a peg-hole which can afterwards be closed, and in less than a year it will be fit to bottle.

SMALL WHITE MEAD

Take three gallons of spring water, make it hot, and dissolve in it three quarts of honey, and one pound of loaf sugar. Let it boil about one-half hour, and skim it as long as any scum rises. Then pour it out into a tub, and squeeze in the juice of four lemons, put in the rinds but of two. Twenty cloves, two races of ginger, one top of sweet briar, and one top of rosemary. Let it stand in a tub till it is but blood-warm; then make a brown toast, and spread it with two or three spoonfuls of ale yeast. Put it into a vessel fit for it, let it stand four or five days, then bottle it out.

TO MAKE STRONG MEAD

Take of spring water what quantity you please, make it more than blood-warm, and dissolve honey in it until it is strong enough to bear an egg, the breadth of a shilling; then boil it gently, near an hour, taking off the scum as it rises. Then put to nine or ten gallons seven or eight large blades of mace, three nutmegs quartered, twenty cloves, three or four sticks of cinnamon, two or three roots of ginger, and one-quarter ounce of Jamaica pepper; put these spices into the kettle to the honey and water, a whole lemon,

74

with a sprig of sweet briar, and a sprig of
rosemary. Tie the briar and rosemary together, and when they have boiled a little
while, take them out and throw them away;
but let your liquor stand on the spice in
a clear earthen pot till the next day. Then
strain it into a vessel that is fit for it, put
the spice in a bag, hang it in the vessel,
stop it, and at three months draw it into
bottles. Be sure that it is fine when it is
bottled. After it is bottled six weeks it is
fit to drink.

MEAD, METHEGLIN, OR HONEY WINE

Boil honey in water for an hour; the proportion is from three to four pounds to each
gallon. Half an ounce of hops will both
refine and preserve it, but is not commonly
added. Skim carefully, draining the skim-
mings through a hair sieve, and return what
runs through. When of a proper coolness,
stir in yeast; one teacupful of solid yeast
will serve for nine gallons. Tun it, and let
it work over, filling it up till the fermentation
subsides. Paste over brown paper and watch
it. Rich mead will keep seven years, and
afford a brisk, nourishing, and pleasant
drink. Some people like to add the thinly
shaved rind of a lemon to each gallon while

boiling, and put the fruit, free from pith, into the tub. Others flavor it with spices and sweet herbs, and mix it with new beer or sweet wort; it is then called Welsh Braggart.

METHEGLIN

Mix one and one-half barrels of water with as much honey as will cause an egg to rise a little above the water; then boil the mixture to one barrel, skimming off the surface. It will be a fine red or wine color, and clear. Then remove from the fire, and when cold, put it into a barrel, leaving the bung-hole open for several days, until fermentation be over; then stop it close and put into a cold cellar.

MOLASSES BEER

One ounce hops, one gallon water. Boil for ten minutes, strain, add one pound molasses, and when lukewarm, add one spoonful yeast. Ferment.

MORELLO WINE

Take the juice of Morello or tame cherries, and to each quart of the juice, put three quarts of water, and four pounds of coarse brown sugar. Let them ferment, and

skim until worked clear. Then draw off,
avoiding the sediment at the bottom. Bung
up or bottle, which is best for all wines, letting the bottles lie always on the side, either
for wines or beers.

TO MAKE MORELLO CHERRY WINE

Let your cherries be very ripe, pick off
the stalks, and bruise your fruit without
breaking the stones. Put them in an open
vessel together; let them stand twenty-four
hours, then press them, and to every gallon
put two pounds of fine sugar; then put it
up in your cask, and when it has done working, stop it close. Let it stand three or four
months and bottle it; it will be fit to drink
in two months.

MOUNTAIN WINE

Pick out the big stalks of your Malaga
raisins; then chop them very small, five
pounds to every gallon of cold spring water.
Let them steep a fortnight or more, squeeze
out the liquor, and barrel it in a vessel fit for
it. First fume the vessel with brimstone;
don't stop it up till the hissing is over.

MULBERRY WINE

On a dry day gather mulberries, when
they are just changing from redness to a

shining black; spread them thinly on a fine cloth, or on a floor or table for twenty-four hours, and then press them. Boil a gallon of water with each gallon of juice, putting to every gallon of water one ounce of cinnamon bark and six ounces of sugar candy finely powdered. Skim and strain the water when it is taken off and settled, and put in the mulberry juice. Now add to every gallon of the mixture one pint of white or Rhenish wine. Let the whole stand in a cask to ferment for five or six days. When settled drain it off into bottles and keep cool.

NOYAN

Take six ounces of peach kernels, and one ounce of bitter almonds. Break them slightly. Put them into a jug with three pints of white French brandy. Let them infuse three weeks, shaking the jug every day. Then drain the liquor from kernels, and strain it through a line bag. Melt three-quarters of a pound of best loaf sugar in one pint of rose-water; mix it with the liquor, and filter it through a sieve, the bottom of which is to be covered on the inside with blotting paper. Let the vessel which is placed underneath to receive the liquor be entirely white, that you may be better enabled to judge of its clearness. If it is not clear the first time, repeat the filtering. Then bottle for use.

TO MAKE ORANGE WINE

Put twelve pounds of fine sugar and the whites of eight eggs well beaten into six gallons of spring water; let it boil an hour, skimming it all the time. Take it off and when it is pretty cool, put in the juice and rind of fifty Seville oranges, and six spoonfuls of good ale yeast, and let it stand two days. Then put it into your vessel, with two quarts of Rhenish wine, and the juice of twelve lemons. You must let the juice of lemons and wine and two pounds of double refined sugar stand close covered ten or twelve hours before you put it in the vessel to your orange wine, and skim off the seeds before you put it in. The lemon peels must be put in with the oranges; half the rinds must be put into the vessel. It must stand ten or twelve days before it is fit to bottle.

ORANGE, OR LEMON WINE, BOILED

Take five gallons of water, fourteen pounds of loaf sugar, three eggs, the whites and shells, one ounce of hops. Boil together the sugar, water, and eggs; when it has

boiled an hour, and become quite clear, add
the hops and the thinly shaved rinds of six
or eight of the fruit, — more or less, according as the bitter flavor is desired. Let it
boil in all two hours; meanwhile remove all
the peel and white pith of the fruit, and
squeeze the juice. Pour a gallon or two of
the hot liquor on the pulp; stir it well about,
and when cool strain to the rest, and add
the juice. Some people strain off the hops,
rind, and eggs; others prefer their remaining. It is by no means important which
mode is adopted. Work it with yeast, as
the foregoing article, and refine with isinglass dissolved in a quart of brandy. This
wine should be one year in wood and one in
bottles, when it will be found excellent.

ORANGE OR LEMON WINE WITHOUT
BOILING

Take one-half chest of Seville oranges;
they are most juicy in March. Shave the
rinds of one or two dozen (more or less,
according as the bitter flavor is desired, or
otherwise). Pour over this one or two quarts
of boiling water; cover up, and let it stand
twelve hours; then strain to the rest. Put
into the cask fifty-six pounds of good Lisbon
sugar. Clear off all the peel and white pith

from the oranges, and squeeze through a hair sieve. Put the juice into the cask to the sugar. Wash the sieve and pulp with cold water, and let the pulp soak in the water twenty-four hours. Strain, and add to the last, continually stirring it; add more water to the pulp, let it soak, then strain and add. Continue to do so till the cask is full, often stirring it with a stick until all the sugar is dissolved. Then leave it to ferment. The fermentation will not be nearly so great as that of currant wine, but the hissing noise will be heard for some weeks; when this subsides, add honey and brandy, and paste over with brown paper. This wine should remain in the cask a year before bottling.

TO MAKE ORANGE WINE WITH RAISINS

Take seven and one-half pounds of new Malaga raisins, pick them clean, and chop them small. You must have five large Seville oranges; two of them you must pare as thin as for preserving. Boil about two gallons of soft water till a third part be consumed; let it cool a little. Then put five quarts of it hot upon your raisins and orange peel; stir it well together, cover it up, and when it is cold, let it stand five days, stirring

it up once or twice a day. Then pass it
through a hair sieve, and with a spoon press
it as dry as you can, and put it in a runlet
fit for it, and put to it the rinds of the other
three oranges, cut as thin as the first; then
make a syrup of the juice of five oranges
with one-quarter pound of white sugar. It
must be made the day before you tun it up;
stir it well together, and stop it close. Let
it stand two months to clear, then bottle it
up; it will keep three years, and is better
for keeping.

ORGEAT

Boil two quarts of milk with one stick of
cinnamon, and let it stand to be quite cold,
taking out the cinnamon. Blanch four
ounces of the best sweet almonds, pound them
well (in a marble mortar) with a little rose-
water; mix them well with the milk; sweeten
to your taste. Let it boil again for a few
minutes; strain through a fine sieve till quite
smooth and free from almonds. Serve either
cold or warm in handled glasses.

TO MAKE PALERMO WINE

Take to every quart of water one pound
of Malaga raisins, rub and cut the raisins
small, and put them to the water, and let
them stand ten days, stirring once or twice

a day. You may boil the water an hour before you put it to the raisins, and let it stand to cool. At ten days' end strain out your liquor, and put a little yeast to it; and at three days' end put it in the vessel, with one sprig of dried wormwood. Let it be close stopped, and at three months' end bottle it off.

TO MAKE PARSNIP WINE

To six pounds of parsnips, cut in slices, add two gallons of water; boil them till they become quite soft. Squeeze the water out of them, run it through a sieve, and add to every gallon three pounds of loaf sugar. Boil the whole three-quarters of an hour, and when it is nearly cold, add a little yeast. Let it stand ten days in a tub, stirring it every day from the bottom, then put it in a cask for twelve months; as it works over, fill it up every day.

PARSNIP WINE, NO. 2

Take one pound of parsnips cleaned and sliced. When the water boils, put in the parsnips, and boil till they are perfectly tender; drain through a sieve or colander without pressing. Immediately return it to the

copper with fourteen pounds of loaf sugar:
it will soon boil, being already hot, and what
drips from the sieve may be added afterwards; one and one-half ounces of hops, and
boil it two hours. Ferment with yeast; let
it stand four days to work in a warm place;
and tun and paste paper over. It is most
likely it will work up and burst the paper,
which must be renewed. It may be cleared
with isinglass, but will not require any
brandy.

PARSNIP WINE, NO. 3

Take seven and one-half pounds of sliced
parsnips, and boil until quite soft in two and
one-half gallons of water; squeeze the liquor
well out of them, run it through a sieve, and
add three pounds of coarse lump sugar to
every gallon of liquor. Boil the whole for
three-quarters of an hour. When it is nearly
cold, add a little yeast on toast. Let it remain in a tub for ten days, stirring it from
the bottom every day, then put it into a cask
for a year. As it works over, fill it up every
day.

TO MAKE PEACH WINE

Take three gallons cold soft water, four
and one-quarter pounds refined sugar, **one**

pound honey, one-third ounce white tartar in fine powder, ten or fourteen peaches. Ferment; then add six quarts of brandy. The first division is to be put into a vat, and the day after, before the peaches are put in, take the stones from them, break these and the kernels, then put them and the pulp into a vat and proceed with the general process.

PERRY OR PEAR CIDER

Make this according to directions for apple cider. Among the caricatures of the day (just after Perry's victory on Lake Erie, 1813) was one representing John Bull, in the person of the King, seated, with his hand pressed upon his stomach, indicating pain, which the fresh juice of the pear, called perry, will produce. This caricature is entitled " Queen Charlotte and Johnny Bull got their dose of Perry."

PINEAPPLE RUM

To three gallons rum, made by the fruit method, add two pineapples sliced, and one-half pound white sugar. Let it stand two weeks before drawing off.

PLUM WINE

Take five pounds of Malaga raisins, pick, rub, and shred them, and put them into a

Home Made Wines

tub; then take one gallon of water, boil it
an hour, and let it stand till it is blood-warm;
then put it to your raisins. Let it stand nine
or ten days, stirring it once or twice a day;
strain out your liquor, and mix it with one
pint of damson juice. Put it in a vessel,
and when it has done working stop it close;
at four or five months bottle it.

POP, OR GINGER BEER

The principal difference between ginger
pop and ginger beer is that the former is
bottled immediately, the other is first put in
a barrel for a few days. It is also usual to
boil the ingredients for ginger beer, which is
not done for pop. Both are to be bottled
in stone bottles, and the corks tied or wired
down. If properly done the corks and
strings will serve many times in succession;
the moment the string is untied the cork
will fly out uninjured. The bottles as soon
as empty should be soaked a few hours in
cold water, shaken about, and turned down,
and scalded immediately before using. The
corks also must be scalded. On one pound
of coarse loaf or fine moist sugar, two ounces
of cream of tartar, one ounce of bruised
ginger, pour one gallon of boiling water;
stir it well and cover up to cool, as the flavor

of the ginger is apt to evaporate. It is a
good way to do thus far the last thing at
night; then it is just fit to set working the
first thing in the morning. Two large tablespoonfuls of yeast, stir to it one teacupful of
the liquor. Let it stand a few minutes in a
warmish place, then pour it to the rest; stir
it well and cover up for eight hours. Be
particular as to time. If done earlier the
bottles are apt to fly; if later, the beer soon
becomes vapid. Skim, strain, bottle, cork,
and tie down. The cork should not touch
the beer. It will be fit for use next day.
Lemon rind and juice may be added, but are
not necessary.

PORTER

Eight quarters pale malt, six quarters
amber malt, two quarters brown malt. Mash
it twice, with fifty-five and forty-eight barrels of water, then boil with one hundredweight of Kent hops, and set with ten gallons yeast, seven pounds salt, two pounds
flour. Twenty barrels of good table beer
may be had from the grains. If deficient in
color, add burnt malt.

PORTER, FOR BOTTLING

Five quarters pale malt, three quarters
amber malt, two quarters brown malt, burnt

malt to color if required. Mash with twenty-four, fourteen and eleven barrels of water, then boil with one hundredweight Kent hops, and set with seven gallons yeast, three pounds salt. Mash the grains for table beer.

PORT WINE

To ten gallons prepared cider, add one and one-half gallons good port wine, two and one-half quarts wild grapes (clusters), two ounces bruised rhatany root, three-quarters ounce tincture of kino, three-quarters pound loaf sugar, one-half gallon spirits. Let this stand ten days; color if too light, with tincture of rhatany, then rack it off and fine it. This should be repeated until the color is perfect and the liquid clear.

PORT WINE (BRITISH)

1. Two gallons damson juice, two gallons cider, three-quarters ounce sloe juice, one pound sugar, one pound honey. Ferment, then add one quart spirit, one gallon red cape, a little over one ounce of red tartar (dissolved), the same of powder of catechu, one-tenth ounce bruised ginger, one-tenth ounce cassia, a few cloves. Mix well with two tablespoonfuls of brandy coloring.

2. Two pounds bullace, ten pounds dam-

sors, one and one-half gallons water. Boil the water, skim it, and pour it boiling hot on the fruit; let it stand four or six days at least. During that time bruise the fruit or squeeze it with your hands. Then draw or pour it off into a cask, and to every gallon of liquor, put two pounds and a half of fine sugar, or rather more; put some yeast on a slice of bread (warm) to work it. When done working, put a little brandy into the cask and fill it up. Bung it up close, and let it stand six or twelve months; then bottle it off. This wine is nearer in flavor to port than any other. If made with cold water, it will be equally as good, but of a different color.

3. Five gallons cider, one gallon elder juice, one gallon port wine, one and one-quarter pint brandy, one and one-fifth ounces red tartar, one-fifth ounce catechu, one gill finings, one ounce logwood. Mix well and bung close.

TO MAKE QUINCE WINE

Take your quinces when they are thoroughly ripe, wipe off the fur very clean; then take out the cores, bruise them as you do apples for cider, and press them, adding to every gallon of juice two and one-half

pounds of fine sugar. Stir it together till
it is dissolved; then put it into your cask,
and when it has done working stop it close.
Let it stand till *March* before you bottle
it. You may keep it two or three years; it
will be the better.

QUINCE WINE, NO. 2

Twelve sliced quinces. Boil for quarter
of an hour in one gallon water; then add
two pounds lump sugar. Ferment, and add
one gallon lemon wine, one pint spirit.

RAISIN WINE

There are various modes of preparing
this wine, which is, perhaps, when well
made, the best of English wines. The following recipes are considered good:

For raisin wine without sugar, put to
every gallon of soft water eight pounds of
fresh Smyrna or Malaga raisins; let them
steep one month, stirring every day. Then
drain the liquor and put it into the cask,
filling it up as it works over; this it will
do for two months. When the hissing has
in a great measure subsided, add brandy
and honey, and paper as in the former articles. This wine should remain three years
untouched; it may then be drank from the

cask, or bottled, and it will be found excellent. Raisin wine is sometimes made in large quantities, by merely putting the raisins in the cask, and filling it up with water, the proportion as above; carefully pick out all stalks. In six months rack the wine into fresh casks, and put to each the proportion of brandy and honey. In cider countries and plentiful apple years, a most excellent raisin wine is made by employing cider instead of water, and steeping in it the raisins.

RAISIN WINE, NO. 2

Five pounds of raisins, four gallons of water. Put them into a cask. Mash for a fortnight, frequently stirring, and leave the bung loose until the active fermentation ceases; then add one and one-half pints brandy. Well mix, and let it stand till fine. The quantity of raisins and brandy may be altered to suit.

RAISIN WINE, NO. 3

Take two gallons of spring water, and let it boil half an hour; then put into a stein pot two pounds of raisins stoned, two pounds of sugar, the rind of two lemons, and the juice of four lemons; then pour the boiling water on the things in the stein, and

let it stand covered four or five days. Strain
it out and bottle it up; in fifteen or sixteen
days it will be fit to drink. It is a very
pleasant drink in hot weather.

RAISIN WINE WITH SUGAR

To every gallon of soft water four pounds
of fresh raisins; put them in a large tub;
stir frequently, and keep it covered with a
sack or blanket. In about a fortnight the
fermentation will begin to subside; this may
be known by the raisins remaining still.
Then press the fruit and strain the liquor.
Have ready a wine cask, perfectly dry and
warm, allowing for each gallon one or one
and one-half pounds of Lisbon sugar; put
this into a cask with the strained liquor.
When half full, stir well the sugar and
liquor, and put in one-half pint of thick
yeast; then fill up with the liquor, and continue to do so while the fermentation lasts,
which will be a month or more.

RAISIN WINE IN IMITATION OF FRONTIGNAC

For every gallon of wine required allow
two pounds of raisins; boil them one hour
in water. Strain the boiling liquor on loaf
sugar, two pounds for every gallon; stir

it well together. When cool put it in the cask with a moderate quantity of yeast (as last article). When the fermentation subsides, suspend in the cask a muslin bag containing elder-flowers, in the proportion of one quart to three gallons of wine. When perfectly clear, draw off the wine into bottles.

TO MAKE RASPBERRY WINE

Take your quantity of raspberries and bruise them, put them in an open pot twenty-four hours; then squeeze out the juice, and to every gallon of the juice put three pounds of fine sugar, two quarts of canary. Put it into a stein or vessel, and when it has done working stop it close; when it is fine, bottle it. It must stand two months before you drink it.

RASPBERRY WINE, NO. 2

Take three pounds of raisins, wash, clean, and stone them thoroughly. Boil two gallons of spring water for half an hour; as soon as it is taken off the fire pour it into a deep stone jar, and put in the raisins, with six quarts of raspberries and two pounds of loaf sugar. Stir it well together, and cover them closely and set it in a cool place; stir it twice a day, then pass it through a sieve. Put the liquor into a close vessel, adding one pound more of loaf sugar; let it stand for a day and a night to settle, after which bottle it, adding a little more sugar.

RASPBERRY WINE, NO. 3

Pound your fruit and strain it through a cloth; then boil as much water as juice of raspberries, and when it is cold put it to your squeezings. Let it stand together five hours, then strain it and mix it with the juice, adding to every gallon of this liquor two and one-half pounds of fine sugar. Let it stand in an earthen vessel close covered a week, then put it in a vessel fit for it, and let it stand a month, or till it is fine; bottle it off.

RASPBERRY WINE, NO. 4

Take two gallons of raspberries, and put them in an earthen pot; then take two gallons of water, boil it two hours, let it stand till it is blood-warm, put it to the raspberries, and stir them well together; let it stand twelve hours. Then strain it off, and to every gallon of liquor put three pounds of loaf sugar. Set it over a clear fire, and let it boil till all the scum is taken off. When it is cold, put it into bottles and open the corks every day for a fortnight, and then stop them close.

RASPBERRY VINEGAR

This may be made either by boiling down the juice with an equal weight of sugar, the same as for jelly, and then mixing it with an equal quantity of distilled vinegar, to be bottled with a glass of brandy in each bottle; or, in a china bowl or stone jar (free from metallic glaze) steep a quart of fresh-gathered raspberries in two quarts of the best white wine vinegar. Next day strain the liquor on an equal quantity of fresh fruit, and the next day do the same. After the third steeping of fruit, dip a jelly-bag in plain vinegar, to prevent waste, and strain the flavored vinegar through it into a stone jar. Allow to each pint of vinegar one pound of loaf sugar powdered. Stir in the sugar with a silver spoon, and, when dissolved, cover up the jar and set it in a kettle of water. Keep it at boiling heat one hour; remove the scum. When cold, add to each pint a glass of brandy, and bottle it. This is a pleasant and useful drink in hot weather, or in sickness; one pint of the vinegar to eight of cold water.

RHUBARB WINE

To each gallon of juice add one gallon of soft water, in which seven pounds of brown sugar have been dissolved. Fill a keg or a barrel with this proportion, leaving the bung out, and keep it filled with sweetened water as it works over until clear; then bung down or bottle as you desire. These stalks will furnish about three-fourths their weight in juice, or from sixteen hundred to two thousand gallons of wine to each acre of well cultivated plants. Fill the barrels and let them stand until spring, and bottle, as any wine will be better in glass or stone.

RHUBARB WINE, NO. 2

Cut in bits and crush five pounds of rhubarb; add the thin yellow rind of a lemon, and one gallon of water, and let stand covered two days. Strain off the liquid and add four pounds of sugar. Put this into a small cask with the bung-hole covered with muslin, and let it work two or three days.

ROOT BEER

Take one and one-half gallons of molasses, add five gallons of water at 60° Fahr. Let this stand two hours; then pour into a barrel, and add one-quarter pound powdered or bruised sassafras bark, one-quarter pound powdered or bruised wintergreen bark, one-quarter pound bruised sarsaparilla root, one-half pint yeast, water enough to fill the small barrel. Ferment for twelve hours and bottle.

ROSE WINE

Take a well-glazed earthen vessel and put into it three gallons of rose-water drawn with a cold still. Put into that a sufficient quantity of rose-leaves, cover it close and set it for an hour in a kettle or copper of hot water, to take out the whole strength and tincture of the roses; and when cold press the rose-leaves hard into the liquor, and steep fresh ones in it, repeating it till the liquor has got the full strength of the roses. To every gallon of the liquor put three pounds of loaf sugar, and stir it well, that it may melt and disperse in every part. Then put in a cask or convenient vessel to ferment, and put in a piece of bread toast hard and covered with yeast. Let it stand for thirty days, when it will be ripe and have a fine flavor, having the whole scent and strength of the roses in it, and it may be greatly improved by adding wine and spices to it. By this method of infusion, wine of carnations, clove gilliflowers, violets, primroses, or any other flower having a curious scent, may be made.

RUM SHRUB

One gallon raisin wine, six pounds of honey, ten gallons of good-flavored rum.

TO MAKE SAGE WINE

Boil five quarts of water one-quarter of an hour, and when it is blood-warm put five pounds of Malaga raisins, picked, rubbed, and shred, into it with almost three and one-quarter quarts of red sage shred, and a little of ale yeast. Stir all well together and let it stand in a tub covered warm six or seven days; then strain it off and put in a runlet. Let it work three or four days, and then stop it up. When it has stood six or seven days put in a quart or two of Malaga sherry, and when it is fine, bottle it.

SAGE WINE ANOTHER WAY

Take six pounds of Malaga raisins picked clean and shred small, and one peck of green sage shred small; then boil one gallon of water. Let the water stand till it is luke-warm, then put it in a tub to your sage and raisins; let it stand five or six days, stir-

ring it twice or thrice a day. Then strain
and press the liquor from the ingredients,
put it in a cask, and let it stand six months;
then draw it clean off into another vessel.
Bottle it in two days; in a month or six
weeks it will be fit to drink, but best when it
is a year old.

TO MAKE SARATOGA WINE OR ENGLISH SACK

To every quart of water put a sprig of
rue, and to every gallon a handful of fennel
roots; boil these half an hour, then strain it
out, and to every gallon of this liquor put
three pounds of honey. Boil it two hours,
and skim it well. When it is cold, pour it
off, and turn it into the vessel, or such cask
as is fit for it. Keep it a year in the vessel,
and then bottle it. It is a very good sack.

SARSAPARILLA MEAD

One-half pound of Spanish sarsaparilla.
Boil five hours, so as to strain off one gallon. Add eight pounds sugar, five ounces
of tartaric acid. One-quarter of a wine-
glass of syrup to one gill of water, and one-
quarter of a teaspoonful of soda water, is a
fair proportion for a drink.

SCHIEDAM SCHNAPPS, TO IMITATE

To two and one-half gallons good common gin and five over proof, add one and one-half pints strained honey, two and one-half pints clear water, one-half pint white sugar syrup, one-half pint spirits of nutmegs mixed with the nitric ether, one-half pint orange-flower water, one cup pure water, one-tenth ounce acetic ether, one drop oil of wintergreen dissolved with the acetic ether. Mix all the ingredients well; if necessary fine with alum and salt of tartar.

TO MAKE SCURVY - GRASS WINE

Take the best large scurvy-grass tops and leaves, in May, June, or July; bruise them well in a stone mortar. Put them in a well-glazed earthen vessel and sprinkle them over with some powder of crystal of tartar; then smear them with some virgin honey, and being covered close let it stand twenty-four hours. Set water over a gentle fire, putting to every gallon three pints of honey, and when the scum rises, take it off and let it cool. Then put the stamped scurvy-grass into a barrel, and pour the liquor to it, setting the vessel conveniently edgeways, with a tap at the bottom. When it has been infused twenty-four hours, draw off the liquor, strongly press the juice and moisture out of the herb into the barrel or vessel, and put the liquor up again. Then put a little new yeast to it, and suffer it to ferment three days, covering the bung or vent with a piece of bread spread over with mustard-seed, downward, in a cool place, and let it continue till it is fine and drinks brisk. Drain off the finest part, leaving only the dregs behind; afterward add more herb and ferment it with whites of eggs, flour, and fixed nitre, very nice, or the juice of green grapes, if they are to be had, to which add six pounds of syrup of mustard, all mixed and well beaten together, to refine it down, and it will drink brisk, but it is not very pleasant, being here inserted among artificial wines rather for the sake of health than for the delightfulness of its taste.

SHERBET

In one quart of water boil six or eight sticks of rhubarb ten minutes; strain the boiling liquor on the thin-shaved rind of a lemon. Add two ounces of clarified sugar with a wine-glass of brandy. Stir the above, and let it stand five or six hours before using.

SHERRY WINE

To five gallons prepared cider add one quart spirits, three-quarters of a pound of raisins, three quarts good sherry, and a few drops oil bitter almonds (dissolved in alcohol). Let it stand ten days, and draw it off carefully. Fine it down, and again rack it into another cask.

LONDON SHERRY WINE

Twelve pounds chopped raisins, three gallons soft water, one pound sugar, one-half ounce white tartar, two quarts cider. Let them stand together in a close vessel one month; stir frequently. Then add one quart of spirits, one-quarter pound wild cherries bruised. Let them stand one month longer and fine with isinglass.

TO MAKE SHRUB

Take two quarts of brandy, and put it in a large bottle, adding to it the juice of five lemons, the peels of two, and one-half a nutmeg. Stop it up and let it stand three days, and add to it three pints of white wine, one and one-half pounds of sugar. Mix it, strain it twice through a flannel, and bottle it up. It is a pretty wine, and a cordial.

SPRUCE BEER

Boil a handful of hops and two handfuls of the chips of sassafras root, in ten gallons of water. Strain it, and turn on, while hot, one gallon of molasses, two spoonfuls of the essence of spruce, two spoonfuls of ginger, one spoonful of pounded allspice. Put it into a cask, and when cold enough, add one-half pint of good yeast. Stir it well; stop it close. When clear, bottle and cork it.

STRAWBERRY WINE, NO. 1

Twelve gallons bruised strawberries, ten gallons cider, seven gallons water, twenty-five pounds sugar. Ferment, then add one-half ounce bruised orris root, one-half ounce bruised bitter almonds, one-half ounce bruised cloves, six ounces red tartar.

STRAWBERRY WINE, NO. 2

Crush the berries and add one quart of water to one gallon of berries and let stand twenty-four hours. Strain and add two and one-half pounds of white sugar to one gallon of juice. Put in cask, with thin muslin tacked over the bung-hole, and let ferment, keeping it full from a quantity reserved for the purpose. If a small quantity is made, use jugs or bottle. When fermentation

103

ceases, add one pint of good whiskey to the gallon, and bottle and seal securely. Ready for use in six weeks.

ROYAL STRAWBERRY ACID

Take three pounds of ripe strawberries, two ounces of citric acid, and one quart of spring water. Dissolve the acid in the water, and pour it on the strawberries, and let them stand in a cool place twenty-four hours. Then drain the liquid off, and pour it on three more pounds of fruit; let it stand twenty-four hours. Add to the liquid its own weight of sugar; boil it three or four minutes in a porcelain-lined preserve-kettle, lest metal may affect the taste, and when cool cork it in bottles lightly for three days, then tightly, and seal them. Keep in a dry and cool place. It is delicious for sick and well.

TO MAKE SUGAR WINE

Boil five and one-half quarts of spring water a quarter of an hour, and when it is blood-warm put five pounds of Malaga raisins picked, rubbed, and shred into it, with five quarts of red sage shred and one-half cup of ale yeast; stir all well together, and let it stand in a tub covered warm six or seven days, stirring it once a day. Then strain it out and put it in a runlet; let it work three or four days, and stop it up. When it has stood six or seven days, put in a quart or two of Malaga sack, and when it is fine, bottle it.

TEARS OF THE WIDOW OF MALA-BAR

Five quarts of plain spirit at 18°, one-half ounce bruised cloves, forty-eight grains bruised mace. Digest in a corked carboy for a week, add burnt sugar to impart a slight color, filter, and add four and one-half pounds white sugar, dissolved in one-half gallon of distilled or filtered rain water. Some add two or three ounces of orange-flower water. A pleasant liquor.

TOMATO WINE

Take ripe, fresh tomatoes, mash very fine, strain through a fine sieve, sweeten with good sugar to suit the taste, set it away in an earthen or glass vessel, nearly full, cover tight, with the exception of a small hole for the refuse to work off through during its fermentation. When it is done fermenting, it will become pure and clear. Then bottle and cork tight. A little salt improves its flavor; age improves it.

TOMATO BEER

Gather the fruit once a week, stem, wash, and mash it. Strain through a coarse linen bag, and to every gallon of the juice add one pound of good moist brown sugar. Let it stand nine days, and then pour it off from the pulp, which will settle in the bottom of the jar. Bottle it closely, and the longer you keep it the better it is when you want to use it. Take a pitcher that will hold as much as you want to use, — for my family I use a gallon pitcher, — fill it nearly full of fresh sweetened water, add some of the preparation already described, and a few drops of essence of lemon, and you will find it equal to the best lemonade, costing almost nothing. To every gallon of sweetened water I add one-half tumbler of beer.

TO MAKE TURNIP WINE

Pare and slice a number of turnips, put them into a cider-press and press out all the juice. To every gallon of juice add three pounds of lump sugar. Have a vessel ready large enough to hold the juice, and put one-half pint of brandy to every gallon. Pour in the juice and lay something over the bung for a week — to see if it works; if it does, do not bung it up until it is done working.

Then stop it close for three months, and draw it off into another vessel. When it is fine, bottle it.

WALNUT MEAD WINE

To every gallon of water put three and one-half pounds of honey, and boil them together three-quarters of an hour. Then to every gallon of liquor put about two dozen of walnut leaves; pour boiling liquor upon them and let stand all night. Then take out the leaves and put in a spoonful of yeast, and let it stand for two or three days. Then make it up, and after it has stood for three months, bottle it.

WHORTLEBERRY OR BILBERRY WINE

Take one and one-half gallons of cold soft water, one and one-half gallons cider, two gallons berries. Ferment. Mix five pounds sugar, four-fifths ounce tartar in fine powder; add four-fifths ounce ginger in powder, one-half handful lavender and rosemary leaves, one and two-thirds pints British spirits.

BRANDIES

APPLE BRANDY

Take seven gallons of water and boil one-half, putting the other into a barrel; add the boiling water to the cold, with one-half gallon of molasses and a little yeast. Keep the bung-hole open until fermentation ceases.

OLD APPLE BRANDY

One gallon of neutral spirits, one-half cup of decoction of tea, one and one-half pints of alcoholic solution of starch, one-eighth ounce of sulphuric acid. This is flavored with one-fourth ounce of the oil of apples. Color with one ounce of sugar coloring.

BLACKBERRY BRANDY

One-quarter pound essence of blackberry, one quart blackberry juice, one-quarter pound of gum arabic, one small barrel pure spirits.

CARAWAY BRANDY

Steep one ounce of caraway-seed and six ounces of loaf sugar with one quart of brandy. Let it stand nine days and then draw off.

BLACK CHERRY BRANDY

Stone two pounds of black cherries and put on them one quart of brandy. Bruise the stones in a mortar, and then add them to the brandy. Cover them close and let them stand a month or six weeks. Then pour it clear from the sediment and bottle it. Morello cherries, managed in this way, make a fine cordial.

CHERRY BRANDY, NO. 1

For this purpose use either morello cherries or small black cherries. Pick them from the stalks; fill the bottles nearly up to the necks, then fill up with brandy (some people use whiskey, gin, or spirit distilled from the lees of the wine). In three weeks or a month strain off the spirit; to each quart add one pound of loaf sugar clarified, and flavor with tincture of cinnamon or cloves.

CHERRY BRANDY, NO. 2

One of the best and most common ways of making cherry brandy is to put the cherries (being first clean picked from the stalks) into a vessel till it be about half-full; then fill up with rectified molasses brandy, which is generally used for this compound, and when they have been infused sixteen or eighteen days, draw off the liquor by degrees, as wanted. When drawn off, fill the vessel a second time nearly to the top, let it stand about a month, and then draw it off as there is occasion. The same cherries may be used a third time by covering them with overproof brandy and letting it infuse for six or seven weeks. When drawn off for use, as much water must be added as the brandy was overproof, and the cherries must be afterward pressed as long as any liquor remains in them before being cast away. When drawn off the second time, the liquor will be somewhat inferior to the first, when more sugar, with a very little cinnamon and cloves beaten, may be added.

CHERRY BRANDY, NO. 3

To every five gallons of brandy made by the recipe for French brandy add one and one-half quarts of wild black cherries, stones and all bruised, one pound of crushed sugar. Let it stand for one week, then draw or rack it off as it is wanted for use.

2. Two gallons good whiskey, one quart wild black berries, well bruised with stones broken, one pound common almonds, shelled, one-tenth ounce white sugar, one-tenth ounce cinnamon, one-tenth ounce cloves, one-tenth

ounce nutmeg, well bruised. Mix, and let them stand twelve days, and draw off. This, with the addition of two gallons brandy, makes most superior cherry brandy.

CHERRY BRANDY, NO. 4

To every four quarts of brandy put four pounds of red cherries, two pounds of black, one quart of raspberries, with a few cloves, a stick of cinnamon, and a little orange peel. Let these stand a month close stopped; then bottle it off, putting a lump of sugar into every bottle.

CHERRY BRANDY, NO. 5

Take twelve pounds of cherries, half red and half black, mash or squeeze them to pieces with the hands, and add to them two quarts of brandy, letting them steep for twenty-four hours. Then put the mashed cherries and liquor into a canvas bag, a little at a time, and press it as long as it will run. Sweeten it with loaf sugar and let it stand a month; then bottle it off, putting a lump of sugar in every bottle.

LEMON BRANDY

Put two and one-half quarts of water in one-half gallon of brandy. Take one dozen of lemons, one pound of the best sugar, and one and one-half pints of milk. Pare the lemons very thin, and lay the peel to steep in the brandy twelve hours. Squeeze the lemons upon the sugar, then put the water to it, and mix all the ingredients together. Boil the milk and pour it in boiling. Let it stand twenty-four hours and then strain it.

ORANGE BRANDY

Put the chips of six Seville oranges in one quart of brandy, and let them steep a fortnight in a stone bottle close stopped. Boil two and two-thirds pints of spring water with eight ounces of the finest sugar, nearly an hour, very gently. Clarify the water and sugar with the white of an egg; then strain it through a jelly-bag, and boil it nearly half-away. When it is cold, strain the brandy into the syrup.

POPPY BRANDY

Take six quarts of the best and freshest poppies, cut off the black ends, put them in a glass jar that will hold two gallons, and press them in it, then pour over a gallon of brandy. Tightly cover the glass jar and set it in the sun for a week or more, then squeeze out the poppies with your hand, and

115

sweeten the liquor to taste, adding an ounce
and a half of alkermes. Mix it well and bottle it up.

RASPBERRY BRANDY

Raspberry brandy is infused nearly after
the same manner as cherry brandy, and
drawn off with about the same addition of
brandy to what is drawn off from the first,
second, and third infusion, and dulcified ac-
cordingly, first making it of a bright deep
color, omitting cinnamon and cloves in the
first, but not in the second and third infusion. The second infusion will be somewhat
paler than the first, and must be lightened
in color by adding one pint cherry brandy,
with five or more gallons of raspberry
brandy, and the third infusion will require
more cherry brandy to color it. It may be
flavored with the juice of elderberry.

RASPBERRY BRANDY, NO. 2

Take a pint of water and two quarts of
brandy, and put them into a pitcher large
enough to hold them and four pints of raspberries. Put in one-half pound of loaf
sugar, and let it remain for a week close
covered. Then take a piece of flannel with
a piece of holland over it, and let it run

through by degrees. It may be racked into other bottles a week after, and then it will be perfectly fine.

RASPBERRY BRANDY, NO. 3

Scald the fruit in a stone jar set in a kettle of water, or on a hot hearth. When the juice will run freely, strain it without pressing. To every quart of juice allow one pound of loaf sugar. Boil it up and skim; when quite clear pour out, and when cold add an equal quantity of brandy. Shake them well together and bottle.

CORDIALS

CORDIALS

To filter cordials, cover the bottom of a sieve with clean blotting-paper. Pour the liquor into it (having set a vessel underneath to receive it), and let drip through the paper and through the sieve. Renew the paper frequently and fasten it down with pins. This process is slow, but makes the liquor beautifully clear.

TO MAKE ANISE - SEED CORDIAL

Take one-half pound bruised anise-seed, three gallons proof spirit, one quart of water. Draw off two gallons, with a moderate fire. This water should never be reduced below proof, because the large quantity of oil with which it is impregnated will render it milky and foul when brought down below proof. But if there is a necessity for doing this the transparency may be restored by filtration.

BLACKBERRY CORDIAL

Mash and strain the berries through sieve. To one gallon of juice put one pound of sugar. Boil and add one tablespoon of allspice, one tablespoon of cloves. Cook till thick. When nearly cold add one quart of whiskey or brandy. Bottle and seal.

BLACKBERRY CORDIAL, NO. 2

To one gallon of blackberry juice add four pounds of white sugar; boil and skim off. Then add one ounce of cloves, one ounce of cinnamon, ten grated nutmegs, and boil down till quite rich. Then let it cool and settle. Afterward drain off, and add one pint of good brandy or whiskey.

CARAWAY CORDIAL

Take one teaspoonful of oil of caraway, four drops of cassia-lignea oil, one drop of essence of orange peel, one drop of essence of lemon, five quarts and a gill of spirits, one and three-fourths pounds of loaf sugar. Make it up and fine it down.

CARAWAY CORDIAL, NO. 2

Take one gallon fifty per cent. spirit, one-eighth ounce oil of caraway, which you dissolve in ninety-five per cent. spirit, one pound sugar, one pound water. Dissolve your sugar in the water; mix, stir, and filter.

CEDRAT CORDIAL

The cedrat is a species of citron, and very highly esteemed in Italy, where it grows naturally. The fruit is difficult to be procured in this country, but as the essential oil is often imported from Italy, it may be made as follows: Take two ounces of the finest loaf sugar, powdered. Put it into a glass mortar, with sixty drops of the essence of cedrat; rub them together with a glass pestle, and put them into a glass alembic with two quarts of fine proof spirit and one pint of water. Place the alembic in a bath, heat and draw off one-half gallon, or till the feints begin to rise; then dulcify with fine sugar.

This is considered the finest cordial yet known; it will therefore be necessary to be particularly careful that the spirit is perfectly clean, and as much as possible free from any flavor of its own.

CINNAMON CORDIAL

This is seldom made with cinnamon, but with either the essential oil or bark of cassia. It is preferred colored, and therefore may be well prepared by simple fermentation. If the oil be used, one dram will be found enough for two or three gallons of spirit. The addition of two or three drops each of essence of lemon and orange peel, with about a spoonful of essence of cardamoms to each gallon, will improve it. Some persons add to the above quantity one dram of cardamom seeds and one ounce each of dried orange and lemon peel. One ounce of oil of cassia is considered to be equal to eight pounds of the buds or bark. If wanted dark, it may be colored with burnt sugar. The quantity of sugar is one and one-half pounds to the gallon.

STRONG CINNAMON CORDIAL

Take one pound of fine cinnamon bruised, two gallons of clear rectified spirit, and one pint of water. Put them into the still, and digest them twenty-four hours with a gentle heat, after which draw off by a pretty strong heat.

CITRON CORDIAL

Take six ounces of dry yellow rinds of citrons, two ounces of orange peel, one and one-half ounces bruised nutmegs, five quarts of proof spirit, one pint water. Digest with a gentle heat, then draw off ten gallons in a bath; heat, and dulcify with fine sugar.

CITRON CORDIAL, NO. 2

One-half pound yellow rind of citrons, two ounces orange peel, one-third ounce bruised nutmegs, two and one-sixth gallons proof spirit; distill or macerate, add water sufficient, and one-half pound of fine lump sugar for every gallon of the cordial.

CLOVE CORDIAL

Take one-quarter of a pound of cloves, bruised, one ounce pimento, or allspice, two gallons proof spirit. Digest the mixture twelve hours in a gentle heat, and then draw off with a pretty brisk fire. The water may be colored red, either by strong tincture of cochineal, alkanet, or corn poppy-flowers. It may be dulcified at pleasure with refined sugar.

CLOVE CORDIAL, NO. 2

One-quarter ounce bruised cloves, or one-quarter dram essential oil, to every gallon of proof spirit. If distilled, it should be drawn over with a pretty quick fire. It is preferred of a very deep color, and is therefore strongly colored with poppy-flowers or cochineal, or more commonly with brandy coloring, or red sanders wood. It should have three pounds of sugar to the gallon, and this need not be very fine. The addition of one-quarter dram of bruised pimento, or two drops of the oil for every ounce of cloves, improves this cordial.

CORIANDER CORDIAL

One-third pound coriander seeds, one-third ounce of caraways, and the peel and juice of one-half orange to every gallon of proof spirit.

GINGER CORDIAL

Pick one pound of large white currants from their stalks, lay them in a basin, and strew over them the rind of an orange and a lemon cut very thin, or one-half teaspoonful of essence of lemon, and one ounce and one-half of the best ground ginger, and one quart of good whiskey. Let all lie for twenty-four hours. If it taste strong of the ginger, then strain it; if not, let it lie for twelve hours longer. To every quart of strained juice add one pound of loaf sugar pounded. When the sugar is quite dissolved, and the liquor appears clear, bottle it. This cordial is also extremely good made with raspberries instead of currants.

GOLD CORDIAL

Take one pound of the roots of angelica, sliced, two ounces caraway seeds, two ounces cinnamon, a few cloves, one-quarter pound figs sliced, one-quarter pound licorice root sliced, two and three-quarters gallons proof spirit, one-half gallon water. Digest two days and draw off by a gentle heat till the feints begin to rise; hanging in a piece of linen, fastened to the mouth of the worm one-quarter ounce of English saffron. Then dissolve two pounds of sugar in one and one-half pints of rose-water, and add to it the distilled liquor. The above cordial derives its name from a quantity of leaf gold being formerly added to it, but this is now generally disused.

LEMON CORDIAL, NO. 1

Pare off very thin the yellow rind of some fine lemons. Cut the lemons in half and squeeze out the juice. To each pint of the juice allow one-half pound of loaf sugar. Mix the juice, the peel, and the sugar together. Cover it and let it set twenty-four hours. Then mix it with an equal quantity of white brandy. Put it into a jug, and let it set a month. Then strain through a linen bag and afterward through blotting-paper before you bottle it.

LEMON CORDIAL, NO. 2

Take one pound of dried lemon peel, two and one-quarter gallons proof spirit, one quart water. Draw off two gallons by a gentle fire, and dulcify with fine sugar.

LIME JUICE CORDIAL

Lime juice cordial that will keep good for any length of time may be made as follows: six pounds sugar, four pints water, four ounces citric acid, one-half ounce boric acid. Dissolve by the aid of a gentle heat, and when cold add sixty ounces refined lime juice, four ounces tincture of lemon peel, water to make up two gallons.

LOVAGE CORDIAL

Take two-thirds ounce of the fresh roots of lovage, two-thirds ounce of valerian, two-thirds ounce of celery, two-thirds ounce of sweet fennel, one-sixth ounce of essential oil of caraway, one-sixth ounce of savin, two-thirds of a cup spirit of wine, two gallons proof spirit, two pounds of loaf sugar. Steep the roots and seeds in the spirits for fourteen days; then dissolve the oils in the spirit

128

of wine, and add them to the undulcified cordial drawn off from the other ingredients. Dissolve the sugar in the water for making, and fine, if necessary, with alum.

NOYAU CORDIAL

Blanch and pound very fine two pounds of the best bitter almonds and one-half pound of sweet almonds. Add the thinly pared rind of two lemons, three tablespoonfuls of boiled milk which has become cold. Put all together into a jar, and add two quarts of old whiskey. Cork up the jar, and let it stand for six weeks, shaking the jar every day. At the end of that time strain the liquor, and to every quart of the liquor add three pints of clarified syrup, and filter through blotting-paper. The almonds that are strained from the liquor make a nice flavoring for puddings, by putting them into a wide-mouthed bottle and pouring whiskey over them.

ORANGE CORDIAL

Take five pounds of the yellow part of fresh orange peel, ten and one-half gallons of proof spirit, two gallons of water. Draw off ten gallons, with a gentle fire.

PEPPERMINT CORDIAL, NO. 1

Take one gallon and a gill of rectified spirits, one pound of loaf sugar, one tablespoonful of wine, oil of peppermint to taste, water, as much as will fill the cask, which should be set upon end after the whole has been well roused, and a cock for drawing off placed in it.

PEPPERMINT CORDIAL, NO. 2

One gallon of rectified spirits, one in five under hydrometer proof, one pound of loaf sugar, one tablespoonful of spirits of wine, one and one-third pennyweights of oil of peppermint, and as much water as will fill up the cask, which should be set on end.

QUINCE CORDIAL

Pare your quinces, and scrape them to the core. Put all the scrapings into a tureen, and see that there are no seeds among them. Let the scrapings remain covered in the tureen for two days; then put them into a linen bag and squeeze out all the juice. Measure it and mix it with an equal quantity of white brandy. To each pint of the mixture add one-half pound of loaf sugar and a little cinnamon and cloves. Put it into a jug and let it infuse for two months. Drain it through blotting-paper and then bottle it. This cordial improves with age and is excellent.

ROSE CORDIAL

Take one pound of the leaves of full-blown red roses. Put them into one quart of luke-warm water, and let them infuse for two days in a covered vessel. Then squeeze them through a linen bag, to press out all the liquid, and take as much white brandy as you have of the decoction of roses. To one pint of the infusion add one-half pound of loaf sugar, and a very small quantity of co-riander and cinnamon. Put in a jug and let it set for two weeks, then filter it through blotting-paper, and put it into bottles.

RASPBERRY CORDIAL

Take one quart of raspberry juice and one-half pint of cherry juice, the fruit hav-ing been squeezed through a linen bag after the cherries have been stoned. Mix the juices together, and dissolve in them two pounds of loaf sugar. Then add two quarts of French brandy. Put it into a jug and let

it stand five weeks. Afterward strain it and
bottle for use.

STRAWBERRY OR RASPBERRY COR-DIAL

Sugar down the berries overnight, using
more sugar than you would for the table,
about half as much again. In the morning
lay them in a hair sieve over the basin; let
them remain until evening, so as to thor-oughly drain. Then put the juice in a thick
flannel bag; let it drain all night, being care-ful not to squeeze it, as that takes out the
brightness and clearness. All this should be
done in a cool cellar, or it will be apt to sour.
Add brandy in the proportion of one-third
the quantity of juice, and as much more
sugar as the taste demands. Bottle it
tightly. It will keep six or eight years, and
is better at last than at first.

WHISKEY CORDIAL

Take one ounce of cinnamon, one ounce of
ginger, one ounce of coriander seed, one-half
ounce of mace, one-half ounce of cloves, one-half ounce of cubebs. Add three gallons of
proof spirit and two and one-half quarts of
water, and distill. Now tie up one and one-third ounces of English saffron, one pound

of raisins (stoned), one pound dates, three ounces licorice root. Let these stand twelve hours in two and one-half quarts of water; strain, and add it to the above. Dulcify the whole with fine sugar.

LIQUEURS

ANISETTE DE BOURDEAUX

Take nine ounces sugar, six drops aniseed. Rub them together, and add, by degrees, two pints spirits of wine, four pints water. Filter.

CRÊME DES BARBADOES

Take one dozen middling sized lemons, three large citrons, fourteen pounds loaf sugar, one-quarter pound fresh balm leaves, five quarts spirits of wine, seven quarts of water. Cut lemons and citrons in thin slices and put them into a cask, pour upon them the spirit of wine, bung down close, and let it stand ten days or a fortnight; then break the sugar, and boil it for one-half hour in the water, skimming it frequently. Then chop the balm leaves, put them into a large pan, and pour upon them the boiling liquor, and let it stand till quite cold; then strain it through a lawn sieve, and put it to the spirits, etc., in the cask. Bung down close, and in a fortnight draw it off. Strain it through a jelly-bag and let remain to fine; then bottle it.

CRÊME DE NOYAU DE MARTI-NIQUE

Take twenty pounds of loaf sugar, three gallons of spirit of wine, three pints of orange-flower water, one and one-quarter pounds of bitter almonds, two drams of essence of lemon, four and one-half gallons of water. The produce will exceed eight gallons. Put two pounds of the loaf sugar into a jug or can, pour upon it the essence of lemon, and one quart of the spirit of wine. Stir till the sugar is dissolved, and the essence completely incorporated. Bruise the almonds and put them into a four-gallon stone bottle or cask, add the remainder of the spirit of wine, and the mixture from the jug or can. Let it stand a week or ten days, shaking it frequently. Then add the remainder of the sugar, and boil it in the four and one-half gallons of water for three-quarters of an hour, taking off the scum as it rises. When cold, put it in a cask; add the spirit, almonds, etc., from the stone bottle, and lastly the orange-water. Bung it down close and let it stand three weeks or a month; then strain it off in a jelly-bag, and when fine, bottle it off. When the pink is wanted, add cochineal, in powder, at the rate of one-half dram or two scruples to one quart.

CRÊME D'ORANGE OF SUPERIOR FLAVOR

Take one dozen middling sized oranges, one and one-quarter pints orange-flower water, six pounds loaf sugar, two and two-thirds quarts spirit of wine, one-half ounce tincture of saffron, four and two-thirds quarts water. Cut the oranges in slices, put them in a cask, add the spirit and orange-flower water, let it stand a fortnight. Then boil the sugar in the water for one-half hour, pour it out, and let it stand till cold; then add it to the mixture in the cask, and put in the tincture of saffron. Let it remain a fortnight longer; then strain, and proceed as directed in the recipe for Crême de Barbadoes, and a very fine cordial will be produced.

EAU DE BARBADOES

Take one ounce of fresh orange peel, four ounces of fresh lemon peel, one dram coriander, four pints proof spirit. Distill in a bath heat, and add white sugar in powder.

EAU DE BIGARADE

Take the outer or yellow part of the peels of seven bigarades (a kind of orange), one-quarter ounce of nutmegs, one-eighth ounce of mace, one-half gallon of fine proof spirit,

one quart of water. Digest all these together two days in a close vessel, after which
draw off a gallon with a gentle fire, and dulcify with fine sugar.

EAU DEVINE

Take one-half gallon of spirit of wine,
one-half dram essence of lemons and one-half
dram essence of bergamot. Distill in a bath
heat, add two pounds sugar, dissolved in one
gallon of pure water, and lastly two and one-
half ounces of orange-flower water.

ELEPHANT'S MILK

Take two ounces gum benzoin, one pint
spirit of wine, two and one-half pints boiling
water. When cold, strain and add one and
one-half pounds sugar.

HUILE DE VENUS

Take six ounces of flowers of wild carrot,
picked, ten pints spirit of wine. Distill in
a bath heat. To the spirit add as much
syrup of capillaire; it may be colored with
cochineal.

LIGNODELLA

Take the thin peel of three oranges and
three lemons; steep them in one-half gallon
of brandy or rum, close stopped **for two or**

three days. Then take three quarts of water and one and one-half pounds of loaf sugar clarified with the whites of two eggs. Let it boil one-quarter hour, then strain it through a fine sieve, and let it stand till cold; strain the brandy with the peels, add the juice of three oranges and five lemons to each gallon. Keep it close stopped up five weeks, then bottle it.

MARASCHINO

One gallon proof whiskey, two quarts of water, dissolve four pounds of sugar, one-third dram oil of bergamot, one-third dram oil of cloves, two drops oil of cinnamon, two-thirds ounce of nutmegs, bruised, five ounces of orange peel, one ounce of bitter almonds, bruised, one-third dram oil of lemon. Dissolve the oil in alcohol; color with cochineal and burnt sugar.

MARASQUIN DE GROSEILLES

Take eight and one-half pounds of gooseberries, quite ripe, one pound black cherry leaves. Bruise and ferment; distill and rectify the spirits. To each pint of this spirit add as much distilled water, and one pound of sugar.

NECTAR

Take three gallons of red ratafia, one-quarter ounce of cassia-oil, and an equal quantity of the oil of caraway seeds. Dissolve in a little spirit of wine, and make up with orange wine so as to fill up the jug. Sweeten, if wanted, by adding a small lump of sugar in the glass.

NOYAU

Take one and one-half gallons of French brandy, one in five, six ounces of the best French prunes, two ounces of celery, three ounces of the kernels of apricots, nectarines, and peaches, and one ounce of bitter almonds, all gently bruised, two pennyweights of essence of orange peel, two pennyweights of essence of lemon peel, one and one-half pounds of loaf sugar. Let the whole stand ten days or a fortnight. Then draw off, and add to the clear noyau as much rose-water as will make up to two gallons.

RATAFIA

This is a liquor prepared from different kinds of fruits, and is of different colors, according to the fruits made use of. These fruits should be gathered when in their greatest perfection, and the largest and most

beautiful of them chosen for the purpose.
The following is the method for making red
ratafia, fine and soft: Take twelve pounds
of the black-heart cherries, two pounds black
cherries, one and one-half pounds raspberries, one and one-half pounds strawberries.
Pick the fruit from their stalks, and bruise
them, in which state let them continue twelve
hours; then press out the juice, and to every
pint of it add one-half pound of sugar.
When the sugar is dissolved, run the whole
through the filtering-bag, and add to it
three pints of proof spirit. Then take two
ounces of cinnamon, two ounces mace, one
dram cloves. Bruise these spices, put them
into an alembic with one-half gallon of proof
spirit and one quart of water, and draw off
a gallon with a brisk fire. Add as much of
the spicy spirit to the red ratafia as will
render it agreeable; about one-quarter is the
usual proportion.

RATAFIA, NO. 2

Ratafia may be made with the juice of
any fruit. Take six quarts cherry juice and
two pounds sugar, which you dissolve in the
juice. Steep in five quarts brandy ten days.
One dram cinnamon, twelve cloves, eight
ounces peach leaves, four ounces bruised

cherry kernels. Filter, mix both liquids, and filter again.

RATAFIA, NO. 3

Take four ounces of nutmegs, five pounds of bitter almonds, nine pounds Lisbon sugar, five grains ambergris. Infuse these ingredients three days in five gallons of proof spirit, and filter it through a flannel bag for use. The nutmegs and bitter almonds must be bruised, and the ambergris rubbed with the Lisbon sugar in a marble mortar, before they are infused in the spirit.

RATAFIA D'ANGELIQUE

Take one-half dram of angelica seed, two ounces stalks of angelica, two ounces bitter almonds, blanched, six pints proof spirit, one pound white sugar. Digest, strain, and filter.

RATAFIA DE BRON DE NOIX

Take sixty young walnuts whose shells are not yet hardened, four pints brandy, twelve ounces sugar, fifteen grains mace, fifteen grains cinnamon, fifteen grains cloves. Digest for two or three months, press out the liquor, filter, and keep it for two or three years.

TO MAKE RATAFIA DE CAFÉ

Take one-half pound of roasted coffee, ground, two quarts proof spirit, ten ounces sugar. Digest for a week.

RATAFIA DE CASSIS

Take three pounds of ripe black currants, one-quarter dram cloves, one-quarter dram cinnamon, nine pints proof spirit, one and three-quarters pounds sugar. Digest for a fortnight.

RATAFIA DES CERISES

Take four pounds morello cherries, with their kernels bruised, four pints proof spirit. Digest for a month, strain with expression, and then add three-quarters pound of sugar.

RATAFIA DE CHOCOLAT

Take one pound Curacoa cocoanuts roasted, one-half pound West India cocoanuts, roasted, one gallon proof spirit. Digest for a fortnight, strain, and then add one and one-half pounds sugar, thirty drops tincture of vanilla.

DRY OR SHARP RATAFIA

Take fifteen pounds of cherries, fifteen pounds of gooseberries, three and one-half pounds mulberries, five pounds raspberries. Pick all these fruits clean from their stalks, etc., bruise them, and let them stand twelve hours, but do not suffer them to ferment. Press out the juice, and to every pint add three ounces of sugar. When the sugar is dissolved, run it through the filtering bag, and to every five pints of liquor add four pints of proof spirit, together with the same proportion of spirit drawn from spices.

RATAFIA DE GRENOBER

Take two pounds of small wild black cherries, with their kernels bruised, one gallon proof spirit. Digest for a month, strain, and add two pounds of sugar. A little citron peel may also be added at pleasure.

RATAFIA DE NOYAU

Take of peach or apricot kernels, with their shells bruised, in number one hundred and twenty, four pints proof spirit, ten ounces sugar. Some reduce the spirit of wine to proof ·with the juice of apricots or peaches, to make this liquor.

RATAFIA D'ECORCES D'ORANGES

Take two ounces of fresh peel of Seville oranges, one-half gallon proof spirit, one-half pound sugar. Digest for six hours.

RATAFIA DE THURO D'ORANGES

Take two pounds of fresh flowers of orange-tree, one gallon proof spirit, one and one-half pounds of sugar. Digest for six hours.

RATAFIA A LA VIOLETTE

Take two drams Florentine orris root, one ounce archel, four pints spirit of wine. Digest, strain, and add four pounds sugar.

USQUEBAUGH, NO. 1

Usquebaugh is a strong compound liquor, chiefly taken by the dram. It is made in the highest perfection at Drogheda, in Ireland. The following are the ingredients: Take two quarts of best brandy, one-half pound raisins, stoned, one-half ounce nutmegs, one-half ounce cardamoms, one-quarter ounce saffron, rind of one-half Seville orange, one-half pound brown sugar candy. Shake these well every day for at least fourteen days, and it will at the expiration of that time be ready to be fined for use.

USQUEBAUGH, NO. 2

Take one ounce of nutmegs, one ounce of cloves, one. ounce of cinnamon, two ounces of the seed of anise, two ounces of the seed of caraway, two ounces of the seed of coriander, one-quarter pound of licorice root sliced. Bruise the seeds and spices, and put them together with the licorice, into the still with five and one-half gallons of proof spirit, and one gallon of water. Distill with a pretty brisk fire. As soon as the still begins to work to the nozzle of the worm, take one-quarter ounce of English saffron, tied up in a cloth that the liquor may run through it, and extract all its tincture. When the operation is finished, sweeten with fine sugar. This liquor may be much improved by the following additions: Digest two pounds of stoned raisins, one and one-half pounds of dates, one pound of sliced licorice root, in one gallon of water, for twelve hours. When the liquor is strained off, and has deposited all sediment, decant it gently into a vessel containing the usquebaugh.

THE END.

Index

149

Index

Index

Index

Index

Index

Index

Index